Five Ships West
The Story of Magellan

Five Ships West
The Story of Magellan

BY CHARLES E. ISRAEL

illustrated with prints and maps

The Macmillan Company, New York

Collier-Macmillan Limited, London

For my goddaughters, Sarah and Alice

Contents

Ferdinand Magellan

A Skirmish and a Blood Brother

MORNING came abruptly to the harbor of Malacca, as it does in the tropics. One moment the Portuguese ships were surrounded by clammy darkness, the next they rode at anchor in broad daylight.

Four of the five ships were great ungainly galleons. The fifth was a caravel: smaller, lighter, with a high bow and twin towers rising from her stern.

On the caravel, watching the sun rise, stood two men, cousins, each in his twenty-ninth year, each a veteran officer in the service of Manuel, the Portuguese king. The taller officer was Francisco Serrano: quick, bright, soft-spoken. His companion was short but powerfully built, with a swarthy complexion and dark, brooding eyes. His name was Ferdinand Magellan.

The two men were part of an expedition commanded

by one of King Manuel's favorites, Diogo Lopes de Sequiera. Early in the year 1509 Sequiera had sailed from Lisbon, bound for the East Indies, the fabulous Pacific islands of which Malacca was one.

It was not the first of such expeditions. A number of Portuguese ships had already made the voyage around the tip of Africa and set up fortresses and trading posts on the east coast of that continent. Some had traveled even farther to plant the Portuguese flag at Calicut and Cochin, in what is now India. But very few ships had ever ventured as far east as this expedition.

The purpose of Captain General Sequiera's mission was twofold. King Manuel expected him to bring back as much information as possible about the little-known lands of the East. Sequiera would make observations and collect data about the people, their customs, and the cities and towns in which they lived. He would make detailed notes about sailing conditions in the region: charts of the coastlines and harbors, descriptions of winds, tides, and currents. All of this would be valuable to future voyagers.

Sequiera's second task was equally important: trade. The fleet brought with it quantities of copper and glass, commodities common in Europe, to exchange for cargoes of rare and costly dyes, drugs, and spices.

Malacca, where the five ships now lay at anchor, was a jeweled city situated on the northeast shore of the strait which still bears its name. Arab traders had reached it long before and had converted its Malay people to the religion of Mohammed, so that among the palm trees were many richly decorated mosques. Malacca's wealthy inhabitants lived in luxurious mansions with spacious gardens. And on a hilltop, more splendid than any other building, stood the gleaming marble palace of the sultan, the city's ruler.

When the Portuguese arrived the day before, they had been cordially received by the Sultan of Malacca. He had given Sequiera rich gifts and had said he would be delighted to trade with the fleet.

Now, on the second day, everything seemed to be going smoothly. Magellan and Serrano watched boats being lowered from the four galleons and rowed to a large pier where sacks of pepper, worth a fortune in Europe, were stacked and waiting. Then, as the sun climbed higher, swarms of small native craft carrying fresh fruit and fish put out from shore and clustered about the galleons. Nimble Malays clambered up the ropes and began to bargain with the Portuguese. Everyone on board was relaxed and jovial.

Everyone except one person. Garcia de Sousa, captain of the caravel, had spent many years in Cochin and Calicut. He knew that the people of the Orient were far from happy about the Europeans who had been pouring into their lands and in some cases waging war against them. Sousa did not trust the Malays. He refused to allow the peddlers aboard his ship. He watched sourly as more and more canoes closed in around the galleons.

Then, late in the morning, he summoned Magellan

and Serrano to his cabin. He said to Serrano, "You speak many languages. Can you make yourself understood in this city?"

Serrano hesitated. "That is difficult to say, sir. I have not yet been ashore."

"Go now," Sousa ordered. "Take your cousin with you. Find someone who will talk freely to you. Question him."

"About what?" Magellan asked.

Sousa turned and glared at the young officer. "If you were a little more patient," he said, "and a little less blunt when speaking to your superiors, by now you would probably be captain of a ship." His expression was stern as he again addressed the two men. "Gentlemen, my experience has led me to suspect that the people of this city could be less friendly than they seem. If that is so, there will be trouble. We must be ready for it when it comes. I want you to find out if my suspicions are correct."

"Have you any suggestion, sir," Serrano inquired politely, "as to how we can convince anyone in a strange city to give us the information you wish?"

Sousa's reply was curt. "That is your concern."

"We shall do it," Magellan said, his tone as curt as the captain's. He saluted, turned, and strode briskly from the cabin. Serrano followed.

The two officers conferred briefly and devised a course of action for carrying out Sousa's order. First Magellan went to the ship's trading stores and took out half a dozen small bars of copper. He placed these in a pouch which he hung from his sword belt. Then he and Serrano lowered the caravel's skiff and began to row across the harbor.

The morning breeze had died down. Malacca was sweltering under midday heat. Magellan and Serrano moored the skiff at the city's main wharf and strolled through the narrow waterfront streets, pretending to look at the sights. In reality they were waiting for a chance to put their plan into operation.

Serrano spoke Arabic to everyone they met. It was a language he knew well, but beyond that he and Magellan reasoned that a man who spoke Arabic rather than the native Malay would be more likely to act friendly to foreigners. Some of the people Serrano addressed looked blank or made signs that they did not understand. Others replied courteously in Arabic but did not seem anxious to go on with the conversation.

Magellan and Serrano wandered around the lower district of the city for over an hour. By now the heat was almost unbearable. They saw fewer and fewer people, as most of the city's population deserted the streets during the hottest part of the day. The cousins were growing weary and beginning to despair of being able to carry out their mission.

They passed from one of the broad avenues into a tiny alley barely wide enough for the two of them to walk side by side. After they had gone a dozen paces, a man stepped out of a doorway and stood before them, barring their passage. He was filthy, and his face and hands were covered with great ugly sores. He spat at the feet of the two officers. From the rags draped around his body he drew a wicked-looking knife.

Serrano spoke to the man calmly in Arabic, asking him to let them pass. The man spat again and replied, also in Arabic, "Give me your valuables."

Magellan approached the man carefully, until they were standing only inches apart. The man raised his knife in a threatening gesture; with stunning swiftness Magellan seized his arm and twisted it. The knife fell to the ground. The man tried to run, but Magellan held him fast. A furious torrent of words poured from the man's lips.

"He says," Serrano reported to Magellan, "that we'll be sorry we attacked him. He says that before the day is over we'll wish we had friends."

Magellan glanced at Serrano. This could be the opportunity they had been seeking. "Ask him what he means."

Serrano did, but the man shook his head. He seemed suddenly frightened.

Still holding the other's arm, Magellan reached into his pouch with his free hand and drew out a gleaming bar of copper. The man's eyes grew wide. Magellan released him and waited tensely to see if he would run. The man remained where he was, staring greedily at the copper.

Serrano and the man conversed rapidly. Then Serrano said to his cousin, "He'll tell us what we want to know for five bars of copper."

"Four," said Magellan.

Serrano relayed this to the man, who protested loudly. Magellan shrugged and began to walk away. The man ran after him, babbling.

"He agrees to four bars," Serrano said.

The man looked around carefully, then spoke to Serrano in a whisper for several minutes. When he fell silent once more, Serrano nodded to Magellan, who handed over four bars of copper. The informer concealed the copper under his ragged clothes and scurried away, leaving the cousins alone in the alley.

Serrano's face was drawn. "If what he says is true, Captain Sousa's suspicions—" He paused and looked around cautiously.

Magellan took his cousin's arm. They returned to the broad avenue, where there was less chance of their being overheard. "Tell me now," Magellan said.

Serrano repeated what the informer had told him. The seeming friendliness of the Malays was all part of a scheme masterminded by the sultan, who intended to wait until he had placed enough men aboard the Portuguese ships, then move in for an easy takeover. He planned to kill or capture the sailors who were now ashore. By evening every member of the Portuguese expedition would be dead or in prison. "The signal for the attack," Serrano concluded, "will be a column of smoke rising from the roof of the sultan's palace."

The cousins hastened back to the wharf where they had left the skiff. At the far end of the dock laborers were still loading sacks of spices onto the Portuguese boats.

Everything appeared as peaceful as before. Perhaps the informer had lied. It hardly seemed possible that the laughing, chattering Malays intended any treachery. But the two officers knew they could not afford to trust appearances. They must act quickly and carefully. "You go back," Serrano said to Magellan. "I shall stay here on the dock, where I can see and hear what goes on. If I notice anything out of the ordinary, I can signal you at once."

For a moment Magellan did not reply. He was not pleased with his companion's suggestion. He had grown up with Serrano; not only were the two men cousins, they had long ago declared their blood brotherhood, sworn to protect each other even at the risk of death. If the informer had spoken the truth about the sultan's plan and the Malays had indeed been instructed to kill or capture the Portuguese on shore, Serrano might die with them. "No, Francisco," Magellan said finally. "You return to the caravel. I shall stay here."

"How will you know what the people here are saying?"

It was a logical question. Magellan did not have Serrano's skill with languages. But he was still unwilling to desert his cousin. He said stubbornly, "I will not leave."

Serrano gazed steadily at him. "Then you would have both of us die, and all the others, too?"

Magellan reflected a moment. Above all he was a sensible man. He knew this was a moment when personal loyalties were less important than quick, decisive action. He must return to the ship at once. He jumped into the skiff, cast off, and rowed with rapid, powerful strokes toward the caravel. He climbed aboard and reported to his captain.

When Magellan had finished his account, Sousa frowned and glanced around the harbor toward each of the Portuguese ships. "You will proceed immediately to the flagship," he said, "and warn Captain General Sequiera. I shall leave to your good judgment the manner in which you deliver the warning. You know as well as I how important it is that the Malays do not understand what you are about."

Taking one soldier with him, Magellan descended to the skiff, guided it through the press of Malay canoes and sampans, and climbed the rope ladder to the deck of Sequiera's galleon.

There the Captain General sat at a shaded table, playing chess with another officer. Three Malays stood behind him, and another three behind his opponent. They were apparently observing the game. So far, nothing alarming. But Magellan's careful eye caught the glint of the razor-sharp *kris* each Malay carried in his belt. The other Malays wandering about the deck were similarly armed. It could be coincidence that all eyes were steadily watching the little group around the chess table. Maybe it was coincidence that every one of the Malays had a hand resting casually on his *kris*. Maybe they intended no harm. All the same . . .

Magellan strolled up to the commander of the fleet

and saluted. Everything depended now on none of the Malays being able to understand Portuguese. Magellan kept his voice free of urgency. Pretending to be making a casual routine report, he told Sequiera everything he had heard. The Malays watched him with interest, but he could tell from their expressions that they had understood nothing.

The Captain General played his part well. Not for a single instant did he display alarm. He yawned, grumbled, and spoke in a bored voice to Magellan. But his words were: "Warn the men on the other ships. Send a man to the maintop to watch for the smoke signal. And be ready."

Magellan did as he was told. A sailor began climbing the mast while Magellan called out to the commanders of the other galleons. His voice was cheerful, but he was instructing them to remain alert. When he returned to stand near the chess table, the Malays smiled at him. Magellan smiled back. Again he wondered whether the informer could have told a false story.

He turned to glance toward the shore. What he saw made him swing about quickly, just as the cry came from the maintop: "Smoke! Smoke from the palace!"

And at once the Malays began to draw their *krises*. Sequiera, however, was too quick for them. He leaped from his chair, dagger in hand, and attacked two of the nearest Malays. Magellan and the other officer lunged toward the rest.

The Malays had expected to have surprise on their side.

A Skirmish and a Blood Brother

They had been sure of themselves, but they were out-
witted by the very weapon they had hoped to use. Even
so, the Portuguese had no easy time of it. The Malays
outnumbered the Europeans, and they fought fiercely.
Magellan found himself battling as many as four foes
at one time.

It was the Portuguese crossbowmen who turned the
tide. The moment the alarm was given, the soldiers
climbed to positions on the foredeck and rained down
volley after volley of arrows on the enemy. Most of the
Malays were killed; only a few managed to leap over
the side of the ship into the water.

On each of the other three galleons, Portuguese officers
and crews were clearing the decks of Malays in similar
fashion.

But the struggle was not yet over. In the canoes and
sampans massed around the Portuguese vessels were at
least two thousand Malays, all armed. If prompt action
were not taken, even the crossbowmen would not be able
to prevent the natives from swarming aboard the ships
and conquering by sheer strength of numbers.

Captain General Sequiera was quick to recognize the
danger. He gave the order for the flagship to slip its
anchor cable. Then he swung the galleon around, had the
gun ports opened, and unleashed a terrifying broadside
on the native craft. The bombardment sank a third of the
enemy boats. There was no need to fire again. The terrified Malays were paddling furiously, intent on putting as
much distance as possible between themselves and the

ships. What might have been a bitter defeat for the Europeans was now nearly a complete victory.

Nearly. There had not been time to warn the Portuguese on shore. And among these was Serrano.

As soon as the Malays had been driven away from the fleet, Magellan dashed for the rail of the flagship. He slid down a rope into the skiff, where the soldier he had brought from the caravel was still waiting, miraculously unharmed. The two men pulled for shore. Magellan prayed he would not be too late to save Serrano.

At first he could not even see his cousin among the figures milling about on the dock. Then, as the skiff drew closer to shore, Magellan saw Serrano surrounded by five Malays, fighting for his life. The two men rowed even harder in their effort to reach their comrade.

Serrano's sword flashed in the sunlight. One Malay went down, rolled over on the dock, and lay still. But another swung his *kris* at Serrano, and the blade found its mark. Moments before the skiff reached the wharf, Serrano fell. Magellan thought his cousin was dead, but then he saw him struggle to his feet. Serrano managed to evade his pursuers and fled toward the edge of the dock. But he was only able to run a few steps before he sank to his knees, blood flowing from a deep wound in his right shoulder. He was wielding his sword left-handed against the encircling foe when Magellan and the soldier plunged to his assistance. The soldier dispatched one Malay. Magellan dealt with two more, felling them with swift dagger thrusts. Serrano himself killed the fourth Malay, using the last of his strength to drive his sword upward into the man's chest.

Magellan and the soldier half-dragged, half-carried Serrano to the skiff. They made their getaway with very little time to spare. More of the enemy were already charging along the dock, shrieking and brandishing their *krises*. But the skiff was out of reach.

The other Portuguese sailors on shore at the time of the battle were not so fortunate. All were either killed or captured.

Francisco Serrano recovered quickly from his wound. As far as he was concerned, the incident was over. Fighting men ran the constant risk of dying. He had been spared. Serrano was of course grateful to his cousin for saving his life. But he would have tried to do the same for Magellan if their positions had been reversed. This was the understanding between blood brothers.

Yet if Serrano had not lived to pursue his own fortunes, if instead he had died on that Malacca wharf, it is doubtful that Magellan would ever have accomplished the feat which was to make his name immortal.

The Beginning of the Dream

IF MAGELLAN'S FATHER had had his way, young Ferdinand would never have set foot aboard a ship. At least not as a sailor.

Pedro Magellan came from an ancient line of Portuguese nobility. The family had once been wealthy, but when Ferdinand was born in 1480, the Magellans possessed only a few modest holdings of land outside the city of Lisbon.

Magellan's father hoped that his son would enter the Portuguese government service and in time become a skilled diplomat, perhaps even an ambassador. The normal way for a boy to embark on such a career was to become a page in the royal court. Pedro Magellan secured a position for Ferdinand as one of the pages to Queen Leonor.

The Beginning of the Dream

It was a lowly job. The boy was expected to run errands, help clean Her Majesty's apartments, assist in the kitchen and in waiting on table—in short, to perform any task he was ordered to do, no matter how difficult or unpleasant. Moreover, he was on call twenty-four hours a day, for whenever the queen or the queen's servants might need him. Officially he had no time off. Actually there were hours, and even whole days, when Ferdinand did not have to work at all. But this did not happen often, and he never knew when his play, sleep, or even his mealtimes might be interrupted by a sharp command.

In return for his labor, a page received an education of sorts. He was taught to read and write and to do sums. He was schooled in history and a smattering of geography. If he showed exceptional promise, the head of one of the government departments might request that the boy be transferred to his service. There he would receive special training, and in time he might take over a responsible position.

Magellan's father had many friends in the Portuguese diplomatic corps. Some of these friends, as a courtesy to the elder Magellan, occasionally invited Ferdinand to their homes, first obtaining permission from Queen Leonor for the boy to be absent from court for an hour or two. If the young page had shown any interest in the work of these men, it is likely he would have succeeded in the kind of career his father wished for him.

Magellan, however, had other ideas. He dreamed of

The boy Magellan leaving home to go to court in Lisbon

service, and of travel, not as a diplomat but as captain of an oceangoing ship. His fondest wish was to lead a life filled with adventure.

It was not an idle dream, nor in the least unusual. These were exciting times. After centuries of ignorance and indifference to anything going on outside its boundaries, Europe was coming to life again, colorfully and energetically.

This revival, which we call the Renaissance, did not happen all at once. It had been growing for some time. One of the main causes of this growth was the series of holy wars known as the Crusades. For several hundred years, starting at the end of the eleventh century, the Christian rulers of Europe had been leading armies against the Mohammedans of the Middle East in the hope of regaining that land for Christendom. The Crusades may not have achieved what they set out to do—in fact, many thousands of lives were lost needlessly—but they did accomplish one thing of value. They brought the people of Europe into intimate contact with the civilization of the Arab world.

The Arabs were famous traders. They had long been sending expeditions to the Orient, even, as we have seen, as far as Malacca. Rich and exotic goods of the Far East were flowing into the Arab cities of the Middle East. The crusaders in turn bought or captured these goods from the Arabs and took them back to their European cities.

There the products of the East created a whole new style of living. Wealthy Europeans were no longer content to wear rough clothing woven from sheep's wool. They now demanded soft and brilliantly colored cloth. And once they had tasted food flavored with peppers or cloves, they spurned unseasoned fare and were willing to pay well to avoid eating it.

Silks, dyes, and spices were only the beginning. From the East also came medicines to cure many diseases, beautiful jewels, rare and sweet-smelling woods.

Someone had to buy all these goods from the Arabs. Someone had to bring them from the Middle East to the kingdoms of Western Europe. Someone had to sell them once they arrived. A new group arose in the society: the merchants. The merchants became rich from their trade, rich enough to develop a taste themselves for the luxuries they were selling. Prices rose, doubled, and redoubled. If a man could obtain even a few hundred pounds of spices, he could sell them in Portugal, Spain, or other European countries for an enormous fortune.

If he could obtain them. He could still buy them from the Arabs, but the Arabs, aware now of the European craving for what they had to sell, charged so much that most of the profit remained with them. The other possibility was for a European to travel to the Orient and bring the goods back himself.

At first the only way open to the travelers was the land route: across Europe and Arabia and on into Asia. This route was long and arduous and soon proved to be dangerous as well. The Arabs had no intention of allowing anyone to cut into their profitable trade with the East. Also, as Mohammedans, they were sworn and bitter enemies of all Christians. Almost every European caravan which set out for the Orient was attacked and demolished.

The people of Lisbon and Seville and London and Paris knew of these hazards, but they continued to clamor for silks and spices, dyes and drugs. The prices they were willing to pay rose higher and still higher. Satisfying this urgent demand became more and more worthwhile.

Since the land route was so risky, it was only natural for the great merchants who sought Eastern trade to turn to the sea. Portugal was an early leader in these attempts to find a sea route to the East. The most famous of the men who first encouraged exploration was Prince Henry, known now as The Navigator because of the many expeditions he sent out along the African coast. Progress was slow. The land mass of North Africa juts far out into the ocean. The small ships which tried to work their way past this bulge of land ran into tricky winds and currents. Many ran aground; others were forced to turn back. When Henry died in 1460, no one had yet crossed the equator in Atlantic waters.

Still, Portuguese captains kept trying. In 1488, Bartholomeu Diaz, having sailed farther south than anyone before him, ran into a brutal storm which blew him even farther. Days later, when he was able to turn and beat his way north, he saw land and gradually realized that it was the tip of Africa. He named it the Cape of Storms.

Portuguese officers in India in the sixteenth century

(The name was later changed by the Portuguese king to the Cape of Good Hope.)

Diaz, his provisions low and his men pressing him to return to Portugal, was unable to go farther. This was left to Vasco da Gama, who ten years after Diaz's voyage sailed around the Cape and reached India. The sea route to the East had finally been established.

While all this was being accomplished under the flag of Portugal, the Spaniards and the English were busy in another direction.

Long before Christopher Columbus, men had begun to suspect that the earth was not a great flat surface but round, and that if one sailed long enough in one direction one would return to the point from which he started. If this was so, they reasoned, it should be possible to reach the East by sailing *west*.

Columbus was the best-known of those who tested this idea. Sailing farther west than any before him, he discovered the islands in the Caribbean. To the day of his death he was certain he had reached Asia.

Those who followed him learned, of course, that this was untrue. Beyond the Caribbean islands they found their way blocked by a huge land mass that most certainly was not Asia: North, Central, and South America. And in 1513, a Spaniard named Balboa caught a glimpse of the Pacific Ocean—as yet unnamed—from a mountaintop in what is now Panama and realized that it was still necessary to cross this stretch of water to reach Asia. But Balboa believed, along with everyone else at that time, that this route was much shorter than the long voyage around Africa.

How then, with a whole continent in the way, were they to get ships into this ocean so they could travel on to the Orient?

An Englishman, John Cabot, tried sailing northward in an effort to find a passage to the Pacific. He failed, but in the process of searching, he claimed Newfoundland and Labrador for Britain. Balboa, leaving his ships on the Atlantic side of Panama, took his men and crossed the narrow strip of land on foot. He reached the Pacific and built light ships with which he actually sailed a little way down the west coast of South America. Bad weather turned him back, however, and he was not able to try again.

Balboa's method might have worked. But leaving ships in one ocean, carrying supplies overland through the jungle, and then undertaking to build new vessels was no easy task. It seemed much more sensible to try to find another way to get from the Atlantic to the Pacific, and so on to Asia—a sea passage through which ships could sail.

Men tried. Starting in 1500, they sailed farther and farther down the coast of South America, but without finding the *paso*, the way through to the Pacific.

So they gave up. They forgot about the *paso* and contented themselves with the already established route: around the coast of Africa and on to India.

The young Magellan, serving as a page in the Portu-

John Cabot

Christopher Columbus

Prince Henry
the Navigator

Vasco da Gama

Vasco Nuñez de Balboa

guese court, grew used to seeing the voyagers—bearded captains and swaggering officers—when they came to present themselves to the king and queen. He would hear their tales of struggle with the sea, of strange far-off cities, of wars and riches. He listened so often to accounts of the journey around the tip of Africa that he came to feel he knew every mile by heart.

As a small boy Magellan only dreamed of going to sea. When he was thirteen he made up his mind to dream no longer. He would make the wish a reality.

But it was not until two years later, shortly after his fifteenth birthday, that his chance came.

An expedition to the East which had been chartered in the name of Queen Leonor returned in triumph. Three galleons stood in the Lisbon harbor laden with sandalwood and dyes; the cargo would bring a handsome profit to the queen and several favored merchants. There was rejoicing at court. The captains of the ships and their chief officers were summoned to appear before the queen and receive decorations.

Magellan was told to stand by in one of the chambers off the throne room in case he was needed for some task connected with the celebration.

In the room, also awaiting orders from his master, was a young apprentice seaman off the expedition's flagship. He was no older than Magellan, but his arms and shoulders bulged with muscles, his hands were calloused, and his face was deeply tanned from months of toil under the broiling sun. He and Magellan began to talk. They liked each other. Magellan told the apprentice of his desire to go to sea. The youth promised to speak to his captain.

That night Magellan told his cousin, Francisco Serrano, who was a page to King John, about his talk with the apprentice.

"If the captain asks you to join his crew," Francisco said, "I should like to go along, too."

"*If* he asks me," replied Magellan.

Two days went by, during which the celebrations continued. Magellan heard nothing from the captain, nor did he see the apprentice again. He began to lose hope that anything would happen.

Then, toward the end of the third day, a junior officer of the fleet asked to have Magellan brought to him. The boy was working in the kitchen at that moment, helping to roast a whole sheep over an open fire. He came before the officer drenched with sweat. The sailor looked him up and down for a few moments before speaking.

"What makes you think you want to go to sea?"

Magellan returned the officer's gaze. "The sea will be my life," he said.

The officer laughed. "Life indeed. And death as well, my young friend."

"I am willing to take my chances."

The officer stopped laughing. "We shall arrange it."

"I have a cousin," Magellan said. "Can you also arrange matters for him?"

"Does he speak with as much forwardness as you?"

"Not often," replied Magellan. "But when he does, he can say what he wants in at least five languages."

The officer laughed again. "We shall see."

A week later Magellan and Serrano were signed on as apprentice seamen in the fleet.

They worked harder than they ever had as pages. They learned how to handle lines and climb rigging. They took their turn as lookouts in the crow's nest. When the ship on which they were serving sprang a leak, they spent long hours in the steamy hold, helping to man the pumps. They were taught how to steer and hold a course. And in their off-watch hours they learned the basic rules of navigation. In time they both became seasoned seafarers.

After ten years of almost constant sailing, Magellan and Serrano were appointed junior officers under the command of Captain General Sequiera. And with him they made the trip to Malacca which very nearly resulted in disaster.

The Dream Builds

AFTER ITS NARROW ESCAPE at Malacca, Sequiera's tiny
fleet sailed back to the Portuguese colony of Cochin.
There Magellan found orders waiting for him. He was
to serve as an officer aboard a ship carrying an assorted
cargo to Lisbon. This did not displease him. Four years
had passed since he had last seen his native land. A short
visit would be pleasant.

But fate intervened. The ship to which Magellan was
assigned met violent storms soon after it started for
Portugal and was driven onto a sand bar near the Lac-
cadive Islands off the Malabar Coast of India. All hands
were saved, but the ship was pounded to pieces by the
huge waves. Only one boat was saved from the wreck.
It was too small to take all the men off the reef where
they were marooned, so the captain decided that he and

his officers should have the privilege of making for the mainland, while the others waited until help could be sent. This angered the common sailors. They distrusted the captain and were sure he intended to abandon them. The tempers of the men rose until they were close to mutiny.

Magellan, as an officer, could have elected to go with the small boat, but when the conflict between captain and crew became fierce, he eased the tension by volunteering to remain—if the captain would swear to send back a rescue ship as soon as he reached land.

The captain kept his promise. Magellan and the men were picked up promptly and returned to Cochin. As a reward for his quiet heroism, and in recognition of his long and capable service, Magellan was given command of a ship.

This meant that he probably would not return home for some time, but it was not a major disappointment. Although he would have liked a glimpse of Lisbon, there was really not much in the city to attract him now. Both his parents had died. The only close relative he had left in Portugal was a brother, and Magellan had not nearly as much affection for him as for his cousin Francisco Serrano.

In truth, he was delighted with the turn of events. He had achieved his ambition of becoming a captain. And he was living the kind of life he enjoyed, a life of action.

Action there was. In July 1511, a Portuguese fleet left Cochin, again bound for Malacca. This time there were nineteen ships, one of them under Magellan's command. The expedition had two purposes. One was to avenge the treachery of the Sultan of Malacca; the second, and more important, was conquest and plunder. This was a brutal age. Force was the only language understood by all. The rich could only remain rich as long as they were also strong.

This time the Portuguese proved to be mightier than the combined armies of the sultan and his Arab allies. The struggle lasted six weeks, and at the end of it the flag of Portugal flew over Malacca. All the wealth of the city, the spices, the dyes, the precious jewels, now began to flow back to Lisbon. But the Portuguese looked on Malacca only as a stepping stone. They knew of the existence of even richer lands to the east: the fabulous Sundas and Moluccas, known as the Spice Islands.

Following the victory at Malacca, it was decided to send three Portuguese ships eastward. Magellan wanted very much to command one of these vessels, but instead his cousin, Francisco Serrano, now also a captain, was chosen. And here began the chain of events which was to have so much influence on Magellan's later life.

Serrano and the other two captains set sail for the Moluccas. After an uneventful voyage the trio of ships reached one of the islands, a pleasant strip of land caressed by blue waters and blue skies and the gentlest of breezes. The natives were as hospitable as the climate and eager to trade with the Europeans. When the Portuguese saw the wealth of spices, their excitement nearly got out of hand. Cinnamon, ginger, cloves, pepper, all guaranteed to bring unbelievable prices in Lisbon, were present in such abundance that it was not even necessary to go on to another island.

In his eagerness, Antonio d'Abreau, the senior captain, became greedy and badly overloaded his ships. All three started back to Malacca, but they became separated during some rough weather, and the caravel commanded by Serrano struck a rock. Water pouring in through the hole in the bottom made the great cargo of spices swell, and the ship split open. Serrano and his men were able to beach the caravel before it went down, but they found themselves on an uninhabited island with little hope of getting off.

After a few bleak days and nights, one of the sailors sighted a junk approaching the island, attracted no doubt by the wreck of the ship. The junk flew no flag, and this convinced Serrano it was manned by pirates. He ordered his men to hide and prayed that the pirates would be curious enough to come ashore. They were, and the Portuguese launched a surprise attack, captured them, then took over the junk.

Instead of sailing at once for Malacca, Serrano turned the junk back toward the Spice Islands, hoping to pick up another rich cargo. He landed eventually on the island of Ternate, where indeed there were ample spices to fill a thousand junks. But suddenly Serrano lost all desire to return to Malacca, or to go anywhere else. Perhaps it was the friendliness of the king of Ternate, and of his subjects. Perhaps it was simply that Serrano had grown weary of fighting and of sailing small ships through stormy waters and wanted the peaceful life he found in this balmy land. Whatever the reason, when the junk sailed Serrano remained behind. He made his home on the island and became adviser to the king.

But Serrano had not forgotten his cousin and blood brother Magellan. He sent him a letter on the returning junk, and as often as possible after that continued to send letters. In that first message he told Magellan that all he had to do to make himself wealthy for life was to come to Ternate with two or three empty caravels and load them with spices.

Magellan would have liked nothing better, but his services were required in Malacca. Although the Portuguese had conquered the city, their hold on it was uncertain, and they were constantly under attack. Magellan fought in battle after battle. Several times ships under his command were sunk. He himself was wounded at least twice.

After two years of this life he was ordered back to Portugal. His homecoming was not as triumphant as he might have hoped. He possessed none of the riches men often took back with them from the Indies. His only real property was a young slave named Enrique, who had been brought by pirates from the Spice Islands to Malacca, where Magellan purchased him. Magellan treated

Enrique well, and the young man grew devoted to him. He understood the brusque manner and speech of his master better than most of Magellan's fellow-officers.

The end of the long voyage from Cochin to Portugal was now at hand. The ship under Magellan's command was entering the Tagus River; Magellan stood beside the helmsman, directing him through the narrow channel and upstream toward the point where the river broadened into a large basin. On the shores of this basin, rising sharply from the water, lay the city of Lisbon. Magellan gazed with pleasure at the steep and winding alleys lacing the sides of the hills, at the grey stone fortress perched on top of a huge crag in the center of the city.

He docked his ship, reported to the authorities, then

Lisbon harbor around 1500

spent the rest of the day wandering around the streets, greeting friends, renewing memories. As one of the terminals for eastern trade, Lisbon teemed with chattering merchants haggling over shipments of dyes and spices. There were hundreds of waterfront taverns where sailors congregated to wait for jobs aboard the galleons anchored in the harbor. Captain Magellan enjoyed being at leisure among familiar sights and sounds.

But his stay in Portugal would be brief. King Manuel was sending an army to Morocco; he hoped to take over the Moorish cities from which were launched the pirate attacks that endangered Portuguese ships passing along the African coast. Manuel needed every available man for this venture, and Magellan volunteered his services.

Magellan was a sea captain, not a land fighter, but for almost two years he fought bravely with the army and in the process almost lost his life. A lance wound in the leg left him with a severe limp which he was to have for the rest of his days.

Yet through all the war in Morocco, Magellan hardly ever stopped thinking of the East. He kept before him a vision of the Spice Islands, the rich and beautiful Moluccas, where his blood brother Serrano now lived. Magellan dreamed of commanding an expedition to these islands, and at the close of the Moroccan war he thought his chance had come. He boarded a ship for Portugal, intent on asking King Manuel to provide him with ships and men to pursue his dream. He did not think he would have much trouble convincing Manuel. After all, if the expedition was successful, a large share of the profit would go to the king. And was not he, Magellan, one of the most experienced sea captains in His Majesty's service? Had he not spent many years in tropical waters, and did he not know the route at least as far as Malacca as well as any other man alive?

A Plea and a Chance

WHEN Magellan left Morocco he was filled with hope and the excitement of his dream. He reached Lisbon early in the year 1517, expecting to leave again in a matter of weeks, bound once more for the Orient.

His expectations were suddenly and bitterly dashed.

Aside from the one short visit, Magellan had not been in Portugal for over ten years. Conditions had changed. Most of the officials who had been in power when he left were either dead or holding posts outside the country. Magellan found he knew practically no one close to the king.

If he had been wealthy, this might not have mattered. He could have given lavish presents to one or two of the king's advisers and obtained an immediate audience with

Manuel. But Magellan was almost penniless. He had scarcely enough money to provide food and lodging for himself and his slave Enrique. And the king received only those persons sent him by his advisers.

Also, Magellan was thirty-six years old, and in those days this was not considered young. His wound bothered him and he limped badly; it made him appear even older than he was. No doubt the royal advisers to whom he spoke thought him too ancient to command a ship, let alone a whole expedition. Moreover, Magellan made no effort to be charming. He had no patience with the oily, smiling style of speech one was expected to use in court circles. He offended people with his curt, sober manner.

His request for an audience with King Manuel was flatly refused. C649531 CO. SCHOOLS

Magellan then went to India House, the government department controlling all matters having to do with Portugal's eastern colonies. He knocked on doors, sat outside offices, all to no avail. Some of the officials laughed at him and dismissed him without even waiting for him to finish his request. A few, a little kinder, at least allowed him to speak, but gave him no encouragement.

The little money he had was running out. He had to find some way of making a living. No one would give him a ship, but he came, after all, from a noble family, and so he was entitled to a position in the king's court. He got it, but it was a lowly position, with a meager salary, a bitter blow to a proud man who had served his king long and well. Magellan became an usher, a job he might have received at the age of twenty if he had not chosen to go to sea.

Again he asked permission to speak to Manuel. Still he was refused. But he was a stubborn man; he was not ready to give up.

One thing that sustained his hope was the letters which kept arriving from Serrano. They did not come regularly; sometimes two would reach Lisbon at once, sometimes a month or more would pass without word. But the letters were long and detailed. Serrano described the Moluccas carefully: the various islands, the climate, the people, the best places to find each type of spice. As a result, Magellan became as knowledgeable about these islands as probably anyone else in Europe. Surely, he thought, sooner or later I shall be able to approach the king, and then it will only be a matter of weeks before I sail from Portugal at the head of an expedition.

Time went by, however, and Magellan was no closer to his audience with Manuel than he had been when he arrived. In desperation, he decided to obtain it by a kind of trickery.

From time to time Manuel spent a day receiving the humbler subjects of his realm, those who had no influence at court yet had some complaint or request to make—usually to do with harsh treatment at the hands of a landlord or an employer or a moneylender. The people who saw the king on these days did not have to be approved first by the advisers. Their names were placed on a list by the court scribe, and they were called forward in order.

Magellan arranged to have his name entered on this list.

When his turn came and Magellan limped across the audience chamber and knelt before the throne, Manuel stared at him, puzzled. With his swarthy, sun-toughened skin, his bristling black beard, his hardened hands, he appeared to be a common man. But his clothes and his bearing were those of a nobleman. What was such a person doing kneeling before Manuel at a time reserved for the small claims of the poor?

Coolly, Manuel asked, "Who are you?"

King Manuel I
of Portugal

Magellan got to his feet. "My name is Ferdinand Magellan. For twenty years I have served Portugal as a sailor and soldier. I have fought battles for the king, and I have been wounded." He pointed to his injured leg. "This is my latest souvenir. I got it in Morocco."

The courtiers in attendance glanced at each other, raising their eyebrows. What ailed this rude man? Did he not know the customs of court address? One was expected to speak to the king with flattering words. One begged for favors. This oaf was acting as if he and the king were equals. They could see Manuel's temper rising.

"State your request," the king commanded.

"I want my salary increased," Magellan said. He named a sum amounting to only a few pennies more than he was already earning. As both Magellan and Manuel knew, the money itself was unimportant, but an increase would be interpreted as a sign of favor.

Manuel replied angrily, "I shall give you an answer at once. A simple answer. Your request is refused."

Magellan was dismayed, but he did not show it. "Then I would ask the king to appoint me captain general of a royal expedition to the Molucca Islands."

The courtiers gasped. Surely this man was mad. Could he not see how furious he was making the king?

Manuel clenched his fists and leaned toward Magellan. "I want to hear nothing more from you!" he shouted. "Leave my presence at once! At once!"

Now Magellan felt his own anger stirring. He had meant no disrespect to the king. He loved Portugal. He

A *Plea and a Chance*

felt he had demonstrated this love with his years of service. Magellan did not feel it necessary to beg, nor was it in his nature to do so. He was asking in a sincere, straightforward manner for the privilege of serving further. Instead of leaving the audience chamber, he spoke again to the king, holding a tight rein on his anger. "It is my greatest wish to take a fleet to the Spice Islands in the name of Portugal, and to bring back cargoes which will greatly enrich the king's treasury. If—"

Manuel did not allow him to finish. "I told you to go!" he shouted. "Leave my presence!"

Magellan's anger faded. In its place he felt despair. It had never occurred to him to doubt that Manuel would grant his request. He was puzzled and deeply hurt by the king's angry refusal. He knew that if he stood before Manuel any longer after having been told to leave that the king might order him executed. Magellan did not care at this point. Sadly he said, "Since the king will not let me serve him as I feel I can, I must ask permission to serve another lord in another country."

Manuel's reply was swift and sharp. "It matters not to me if you serve the devil himself. Only get out of my sight!"

Magellan left the court.

When he had asked Manuel if he could serve elsewhere, Magellan had had no specific country in mind. Portugal was his country. But Portugal had rejected him. He would have to think about leaving.

39

However, he was not prepared to leave Lisbon just yet. There were things he had to do. Though he already knew a great deal about the sea route to the Indies, he felt he wanted to know more. Day after day Magellan went quietly to the record room of India House and studied everything he could find which had to do with navigation in eastern waters. Hour after hour he sat in a musty room poring over charts, maps, diagrams, and logbooks.

His behavior did not attract attention. He was a sea captain, and sailors are usually interested in the exploits of other sailors. Magellan was even allowed to go through the charts and accounts of voyages stored in a special vault and marked secret.

One day, looking through these secret records, he came across one document which made him sit up abruptly in his chair. Magellan did not get excited easily, but at this moment only great restraint prevented him from shouting aloud.

He glanced about the huge, dimly lit room. At the far end of the chamber the guardian of records was working over some charts. No one else was around. Carefully, keeping his excitement under control, Magellan made an exact copy of the paper on the table before him.

Postponing again his departure from Portugal, Magellan next traveled two hundred miles north to the harbor city of Porto, a gathering place for captains and pilots with many different kinds of experience. There he found cheap lodgings for himself and Enrique. He made himself a regular visitor at the taverns and inns where seamen spent their spare time ashore. He asked questions. He listened to the talk swirling about him. And in his mind the plan based on the secret document was taking shape.

But Magellan was a man of action. He knew how to rig and provision a ship, how to judge winds and currents, how to command a crew. He understood enough of navigation to be able to plot a course from one point to another. For the undertaking he was considering, however, he needed the help of someone with deeper knowledge, someone who understood the theory behind maps and mathematical tables.

Such a man was Ruy Faleiro.

Magellan had known Faleiro slightly when they were both pages in the royal court. They met again late one night in a tavern near the waterfront. The two men were exact opposites. Magellan was somber and silent, Faleiro excitable and talkative. Magellan had spent many years at sea; Faleiro had never been a member of a ship's company. But Faleiro was a skilled astronomer who understood much more than Magellan about the theory of navigation. And he too, like Magellan, was unhappy with King Manuel, who had refused to appoint him Astronomer Royal, even though he was well qualified for the post.

Magellan and Faleiro talked the rest of that night and into the morning. They spoke a little of their childhoods, remembering mutual friends. They discussed their careers, the successes and disappointments they had each experienced since the days of their youth. Finally the captain was satisfied that he could trust the astronomer. "What would you say," he asked, "if I were to tell you that I know of a short route to the Indies?"

"Not around Africa?"

"Not around Africa."

"Unbelievable." Faleiro's voice rose. "I would say it was absolutely unbelievable!"

Magellan took out the copy of the secret paper and handed it to Faleiro. It was a map of South America drawn by one Martin Behaim. At about the thirty-fifth parallel of south latitude the map clearly showed a wide sea passage cutting straight through the great mass of land.

For a long time Faleiro sat staring at the paper. Then he looked up at Magellan, a strange light in his eyes. "Come with me," he said. "Come, come, quickly now."

They hurried to Faleiro's lodgings. The astronomer compared the map Magellan had given him with others he himself owned. Faleiro's maps showed no passage across South America whatsoever.

"Perhaps," Faleiro said, "your map is false."

Magellan did not think so.

"Why not?" asked Faleiro. "If this is a true map, why has no one sailed through the passage and on into the great ocean to the west?"

Magellan had an answer for this. Martin Behaim had died in 1507, nine years earlier. The voyage on which he had based his map must have been made several years prior to that. Magellan had found the document buried among stacks of other charts. Somehow the information contained in it had been overlooked and the map cast aside. It would not be the first time something like this had happened.

This was the true *paso*. Magellan had not a single doubt.

Faleiro sat down at his worktable and made some calculations. He asked questions, his voice growing shrill with excitement. Magellan answered, then asked some of his own. The discussion went on most of the day. By evening Faleiro was convinced.

The two men agreed that a chance for fantastic success lay within their reach. They needed only a patron, someone to provide ships and supplies for the great venture.

Portugal, they knew, would give them nothing. Each had been rejected by King Manuel. Neither would dream of approaching him again.

There was only one place to go for help.

The Charter

FERDINAND MAGELLAN arrived in Seville, Spain, on October 20, 1517. Faleiro was to follow within a few weeks. Their mission was to find a Spanish patron to put up money for the expedition to the Indies.

Earlier in the year, when Magellan had returned to Portugal after the Moroccan war, his possessions had consisted of a chest of clothes, his slave Enrique, and very little cash. His situation now was almost exactly the same.

There was one extremely important exception. Before he left Portugal, Magellan had become acquainted with a young man, Duarte Barbosa, who took a liking to the captain. Duarte saw a man of outstanding talents behind Magellan's somber manner and blunt speech. He gave Magellan a letter of introduction to his uncle in Seville, Diogo Barbosa.

The uncle was himself a man of great ability. He had been born in Portugal but had married a Spanish noblewoman and had become a subject of Spain. When Barbosa was a young man, he had been a captain and navigator, commanding expeditions to Brazil and East Africa. Over the years he had become immensely wealthy from the spice trade and was now very powerful in Spanish court circles.

He and Magellan got along well from the moment they met. Barbosa had a daughter, Beatriz, who was also attracted to Magellan, and it was not long before Barbosa consented to give her to him in marriage.

The two men spent long evenings in Barbosa's candle-lit study, which was filled with ocean charts and books about navigation. Their mutual knowledge of the sea gave them much to talk about. One night Magellan confided to his future father-in-law the reason for his having come to Spain: to seek support for a *westbound* voyage to the Indies, by way of the secret passage across South America.

Barbosa was not surprised by what Magellan told him. But he had a surprise for the younger man. "The *paso* you speak of," Barbosa said, "is not as secret as you believe it to be."

Magellan stared at him, unable to speak.

"Its existence is known to a number of people in Spain," Barbosa continued.

Finally Magellan found his tongue. "But surely no one has gone through it."

Barbosa smiled. "No. Although we know the waterway

is there, no one has yet succeeded in passing from one ocean to the other, or even in exploring the waterway for more than a few miles. But I am very much interested in this *paso*. Only last year I put up money for an expedition under the command of a man named Juan de Solis. He had orders to proceed to the passage and to sail through it to the western ocean. He might have done it, too. He very well might have." Barbosa fell silent.

After a moment Magellan asked, "What happened to him?"

"Solis reached the mouth of the *paso*," Barbosa replied. "He went ashore to see what the land was like and was killed by natives. His crew had neither the desire nor the courage to go on without him. They brought the ship back to Spain without exploring further."

Magellan's first reaction to the fact that others knew about the *paso* was one of disappointment, but Barbosa soon persuaded him there was no need for that. Since no one had actually sailed through the passage, Magellan and Faleiro could still be the first men to accomplish it. Barbosa believed so strongly in the younger man's ability that he was prepared to finance the venture, on an even larger scale than the backing he had given Juan de Solis. Magellan was overjoyed. He had found his patron.

However, as Barbosa pointed out, it was not as simple as that. All foreign voyages having anything to do with the East came under the control of Spain's India House, which was set up very much like the department of the same name in Portugal. No ship could sail for the Orient under the Spanish flag without their express permission.

The Charter

If Magellan had had to apply alone for this permission, it is probable he would have received the same treatment he had got in Lisbon. Now, though, he had a powerful ally who understood all the subtle, twisted workings of Spanish government offices.

Sometimes India House would sponsor an expedition on its own. But if it put up all the money, or even the greater part of it, it would quite rightly expect to receive the bulk of the profits. This was not what Barbosa had in mind.

He applied in a very casual way to India House, asking that the officials sponsor an expedition to the Spice Islands under Magellan and Faleiro, and that the route be westward, through the *paso* which Solis had not been able to explore. He phrased his request in terms which did not contain very much promise for the success of the undertaking. As Barbosa hoped and expected, India House refused. But they also said they would have no objection to granting permission if someone else wished to back the enterprise.

This left the way clear for Barbosa to put up the money himself. But this was not precisely what he wanted, either. While he was prepared to risk a considerable amount of his fortune, Barbosa felt that the expedition, to be successful, would have to be larger than any he would be able to finance alone. He needed other partners: wealthy, influential men. He also wanted royal backing for the scheme. This meant getting a charter from King Charles, the young ruler of Spain.

Obtaining both the proper partners and a royal charter

were difficult tasks. But again Barbosa's experience proved useful. He spoke to two very high officials of India House, Juan de Aranda and Bishop Fonseca, expressing his confidence in Magellan. Since he was approaching them not as government officials but as private citizens, he was able, with eloquent argument, to convince them to become partners in the venture. And since they were personally involved, he was sure he could count on their support in convincing King Charles.

Juan de Aranda began to work with Magellan in planning the expedition. Everything seemed to be going well. In a few weeks they would have all the details they needed for a presentation to the king—information such as the total cost of the venture, the number of ships required, the types and amounts of various supplies, and an explanation of the course the fleet intended to follow in reaching the *paso.*

Magellan was truly happy for the first time in years. He was about to be married to a beautiful and wealthy girl. His dream of reaching the East seemed less a dream now and much closer to reality.

Then Ruy Faleiro arrived in Seville. When he heard what had been happening and saw how well Magellan was working with Juan de Aranda, he was beside himself with jealousy. He screamed and stamped his feet like a child throwing a tantrum. He and Magellan were the only partners, how dare Magellan bring in others? Magellan had known his friend was excitable; he had not realized Faleiro could become such a noisy troublemaker. It took a great deal of Magellan's time and energy, which could have been otherwise employed, to soothe the surly astronomer. He managed it just in time, for the meeting with the king had been arranged, and Faleiro's presence was necessary.

Charles received the delegation in his council room. Besides Magellan, Faleiro, and Barbosa, Juan de Aranda and Bishop Fonseca were in attendance.

Fonseca presented Magellan, who explained to the king what he hoped to accomplish. He told Charles of his contact with Francisco Serrano and how he had gained from it a thorough knowledge of the islands without having yet seen them. He spoke of his own personal experience in Cochin and Malacca and Morocco. He did not boast, but neither did he hesitate to explain to Charles why he thought he was the man to lead such an expedition.

The young Spanish king received Magellan's words in a totally different manner than had Manuel of Portugal. Charles was deeply and favorably impressed. He asked Magellan many questions about the Spice Islands—questions about the climate, the kinds of spices which were available, the goods which could be traded in return for the spices. For over an hour the king kept up a running fire of inquiry. Not once did Magellan hesitate over his replies. Charles seemed almost satisfied. But something was obviously troubling him. After a time it came out.

"How do we know," the king asked, "that these islands do not lie on the Portuguese side of the Pope's line?"

It was an extremely important question. Spain and

Portugal had been the two great rivals in exploration and in trade with the East. There had been frequent clashes between the ships and soldiers of the two countries. At one time the hostilities had grown so intense that full-scale warfare might have broken out if it hadn't been for action taken by the Pope. To keep peace between Spain and Portugal, the Holy Father suggested that the world be divided by an imaginary line and that each country be assigned a specific area in which they could trade and set up colonies. The suggestion had been accepted and a treaty drawn up.

Very little was known about the exact location of the Spice Islands. The king feared that these Moluccas were in Portuguese territory rather than in an area over which Spain had been given control. If this was so and Charles was to charter an expedition, Portugal could consider it an act of war.

The men in the council chamber had been sure that the king would bring up this matter. Now it was time for Faleiro to do his part.

Bishop Fonseca stepped forward. "Your Majesty," he said, "we are indeed fortunate in having with us an illustrious astronomer, perhaps the most famous in all Europe. The tools of his science and the substance of what he explains are highly complex. However, we are all aware of our king's powers of intellect and vision, which give him a greater understanding than most men have of even the most complicated affairs. With your permission, sire, Ruy Faleiro will reply to your question."

Faleiro brought out maps and charts. In complete

silence he took out of a cloth pouch a globe representing what men at that time thought was the shape of the world. Then he bowed very low before Charles. "Your highness, after careful study and lengthy consideration, I have reached the conclusion that the Molucca Islands lie wholly in an area which may be claimed by Spain. It will be an honor and a pleasure to show you how I have arrived at this conclusion."

King Charles I of Spain

CAROLVS RoMA NOR IMPERAToR HISPANIARV REX FOELICISS— ATQ CATHOL—

The king listened as carefully as he had to Magellan. He watched Faleiro's nimble fingers moving among the charts and papers as he continued with his explanation. When Faleiro finished speaking, Charles looked around at the men. They waited tensely while the young monarch considered what the astronomer had said.

Then Charles nodded. Royal assent had been given. A charter would be drawn up.

The terms of the charter were even better than Magellan had hoped. He and Faleiro were to be given five ships to take through the *paso* and on to the Spice Islands. The king was, of course, to receive a share of the profits, as were Barbosa, Juan de Aranda and Fonseca, but there would be an ample amount left for Magellan and Faleiro. In addition, no one else would be given permission to follow their route to the East for a period of ten years. And as a special bonus, the two expedition leaders were to be royal governors of any lands they discovered.

Magellan was understandably jubilant, and he was a little puzzled by the attitude of the man who was to be his father-in-law. "Wait, my son," Barbosa told him. "We have come a long way, but we have a longer way to go."

"Of course," Magellan said. "But the most difficult task is surely behind us."

Barbosa shook his head. He had too much knowledge of politics to believe that everything would go smoothly from here on.

Elusive Success

BARBOSA was right. Even before the charter had been put onto paper, trouble was on the way. King Manuel of Portugal, like all European rulers of his day, had spies in every land. His agents in Seville quickly reported to him the plans for Magellan's expedition.

Manuel was furious, more than he might ordinarily have been. It was not so very unusual for a man to change his loyalty from one country to another, but this was a man the Portuguese king had thought of as worthless. He had let him go. Now Spain obviously respected him enough to make him Captain General of a fleet. Manuel instructed his ambassador to Spain, Alvara de Costa, to meet with Magellan and try to dissuade him from setting out on the voyage.

Costa first tried an appeal to Magellan's patriotism.

"You were born a Portuguese," he said. "You will never feel comfortable sailing under the Spanish flag."

Magellan's reply was blunt. "Portugal had her chance. She rejected me."

Then Costa made a foolish mistake. "If you persist in taking command of this expedition," he said, "I will see that you have cause to regret it deeply."

Magellan held onto his temper, but only barely. "If you persist in trying to threaten me, I will break every bone in your body. For your own safety—get out of my sight!"

Costa went to see King Charles. He had no more success with the young ruler than with Magellan. In fact, Costa's visit had the effect of making Charles more eager than ever for the expedition to get under way.

The real trouble at this time did not come from the Portuguese ambassador. It sprang from a source Magellan never would have suspected: Bishop Fonseca. Like many high officials of his time, the bishop had interests extending far beyond the borders of his own country. His fortune, which was considerable, had been amassed by cleverness and not a little double-dealing. Fonseca trusted no other man. He was capable of great ruthlessness in destroying anyone he thought of as a rival. It was his aim to be in complete control of this expedition and to share whatever profits came from it with no one, or at least with as few people as possible.

He first set out to eliminate Juan de Aranda. In the space of a few weeks, Fonseca was able to rig a number of charges against his colleague and to make them sound so convincing that he could persuade the king to dismiss Aranda from all high offices, including his partnership in the expedition.

At the same time Fonseca took steps to get rid of Faleiro. He played on the astronomer's vanity, telling him that he, not Magellan, should be Captain General and encouraging him to quarrel constantly with Magellan. Fonseca watched Magellan's patience grow thin. He waited until he was sure Magellan had had as much of Faleiro's troublemaking as he could stand. Then the bishop went to the Captain General and sympathized with him over his difficulties with the astronomer. He talked Magellan into writing to King Charles, asking that Faleiro be removed from his position with the expedition. The king granted Magellan's request, but this was not enough for Fonseca. Faleiro still retained his contract for a share of the profits. At this point Fonseca summoned all the wiles at his command and actually convinced Faleiro he should give up his claim. In order to accomplish this, he made the astronomer a number of grand promises about future, infinitely richer expeditions— promises he had absolutely no intention of keeping.

This left only two men to reckon with: Diogo Barbosa and Magellan. Bishop Fonseca knew, naturally, of the close tie developing between Barbosa and the Captain General, and there was little he could do about that. But he could see that his nephew, Juan de Cartagena, was signed on as captain of one of the ships. Fonseca went to King Charles. The bishop was too clever and experienced to hint that Magellan might not be a capable commander. Instead he said to Charles, "Sire, I am deeply concerned. While I am completely certain that Ferdinand Magellan has nothing but affection for Your Majesty, he was, after all, originally a Portuguese subject. I am sure, Your Highness, that there is no man better able to captain the fleet than this Portuguese. He is brave, skilled, and determined. But one must remember that he is indeed a Portuguese. Purely for the sake of form, Your Majesty, might it not be wise to provide a measure of control over the Portuguese? A Spanish Co-Captain General perhaps? Now, it is possible that my nephew, Juan de Cartagena, is not the only choice Your Majesty could make for such a position, but he is available, and he would, I am sure, die before he would see Your Majesty's interests betrayed to another country, most of all to Portugal."

And so on and on he went, mentioning Magellan's first nationality at every opportunity. If Magellan had not impressed the king so deeply, Fonseca might have succeeded, and perhaps even before the ships sailed he might have been able to figure out a way to get rid of Magellan and leave Cartagena in complete command. But Charles believed in his Captain General. He refused to do what Fonseca asked. For the moment the bishop had to be satisfied with what he had already achieved, and to wait. Meanwhile, as he continued to plot and maneuver, Fonseca was professing great friendship for Magellan and pretending to help him in every way he could.

The year 1517 was drawing to a close. Magellan confidently expected to have his five ships under way early in the new year, at the very latest by June. He spoke to Diogo Barbosa, explaining that he would like to enjoy at least a couple of months of married life with his beloved Beatriz before he sailed away. Would it be possible for Barbosa to make an exception and forget the customary long engagement period, so that the wedding ceremony could be performed at once? Barbosa smiled to himself. He knew how many difficulties still lay in the way of Magellan's quick departure, but he would not say anything to spoil the couple's happiness. Instead he gave Beatriz and Magellan his permission to marry.

There was little time for a honeymoon. Magellan had already purchased the ships for the expedition, five old galleons which had to be completely refitted. This part of the preparation was tedious, but it was work Magellan understood thoroughly. He supervised the replacement of rotten timbers, the caulking of leaky seams, the strengthening of gun mounts—everything to make certain the vessels were in the best possible condition to withstand the brutal weather he was sure they would encounter. To Magellan, these ships were more than mere collections of wood and metal, hammered together skillfully enough so they would float and keep out the ocean. Each vessel was almost a living thing in the eyes of the Captain General. Each was already developing its own personality. Even while the galleons lay on their sides in the shipyard, Magellan was sure he knew how each would behave at sea—which ones would ride well in heavy weather, which could be counted on to be especially maneuverable, which might need extra skill at the helm when caught in sudden squalls or strong crosscurrents.

Magellan worked long, hard hours, beginning each morning before dawn. But Diogo Barbosa had set aside a special apartment in his rambling, luxurious mansion for his daughter and son-in-law, and there Magellan spent the evenings with Beatriz.

It was just as well he had a little time for relaxation. His problems with the expedition were just beginning.

For one thing, the Portuguese had not given up. They were determined that Magellan, whom they now regarded as an enemy, would never command a Spanish expedition to the East.

Stationed in Seville as Portuguese consul was a man named Sebastian Alvarez. Despite his lower rank, he was a much cleverer man than the ambassador Costa. Alvarez began a whispering campaign against Magellan in the taverns and inns. He was too wise to participate himself. He hired Spaniards, mainly waterfront idlers who were ready to do anything for a few pieces of silver. They went among the captains and seamen, talking about Magellan, calling him a "Portuguese upstart," stirring up jealousy, asking why he had been elevated to a position where he was able to order about loyal Spanish subjects.

At first the resentment against Magellan was confined to talk, but soon the opportunity arose for Alvarez to strike a real blow.

Building a caravel

At that time there were no protective drydocks as we know them today. Ships were beached at high tide and overturned, or careened, when the tide went out, so that work could be done on the hull. One morning while the *Trinidad*, which was to be Magellan's flagship, was being overhauled in this fashion, a crowd collected to watch the work. After a while one among them, a thug paid by Alvarez, pointed to the flag on the mainmast. "Look!" he shouted. "This foreigner, this devil from Lisbon, has the insolence to fly the Portuguese flag on his ship!"

It was not the Portuguese flag. It was Magellan's personal ensign, which, as Captain General, he was privileged to fly on his own ship. But before Magellan could explain this, the troublemaker cried out, "Tear it down! Tear down the Portuguese flag!"

The crowd surged toward Magellan and his men, shouting and cursing. Several sword fights broke out, and Magellan himself was slightly wounded in the fracas which followed.

The harbor guard arrived and restored order but then proceeded to side with the mob and tried to take down Magellan's standard.

Magellan tried to argue politely with the captain of the guard, telling him that this was not the Portuguese ensign. "In fact," he said, "the only reason the Spanish flag is not flying is that this very morning I sent it to be cleaned."

The captain of the guard was stubborn. "Only one flag flies here. The Spanish."

"But I've just told you—" Magellan began.

"The Spanish flag," insisted the captain of the guard. "I don't want to listen to a lot of wind about anything else." He turned to one of his officers. "Take it down."

This was too much for Magellan. He seized the captain of the guard in a vicelike grip. "This ship belongs to the king. You know he will not tolerate having his property tampered with. Take down the flag if you like. But remember. King Charles has had men executed for less."

The captain of the guard considered a moment. Then, rather than risk the royal rage, he grudgingly forced the crowd to scatter and withdrew his men from the ship.

Magellan had no desire to make trouble for the harbor guard. But he knew that, in order to avoid similar incidents, some action should be taken against the culprits. He made a report to King Charles, recommending that the guard be reprimanded. The king responded by recalling the guard's liberty privileges for a period of time, and Magellan had no further trouble from that source.

He had enough other difficulties to contend with, though. The Portuguese had been foiled in their attempt at open sabotage, but they worked diligently and effectively behind the scenes. Never had an expedition taken so long to get under way. Equipment and tools were lost. Work was badly done and had to be done again. Workers quit, and no replacements could be found. Magellan tried to cope with all these obstacles, and when he was personally overseeing a job it would be done well. But there were five ships, and he could not be everywhere at once.

A view of the Seville waterfront in the sixteenth century

The year 1518 wore on, and it was a year of little enough joy for Magellan so far as the expedition was concerned. But there was still Beatriz, and their life together, and in September a son was born to the couple.

Magellan took one day off from his work to celebrate. There was no time for more lengthy festivity. The ships had finally been made seaworthy, and it was time to begin gathering crews.

The hiring of able-bodied seamen at that time was usually accomplished by scouting around in one or another of the many taverns lining the Seville waterfront. Magellan preferred to act as his own recruiting agent. He wanted to be certain that the men who sailed with him would be the very best he could find.

He entered the first tavern—a low-ceilinged room foul with the odors of stale wine, wood smoke, and unwashed bodies. Magellan called for quiet, and in a few moments the talk and laughter stopped. He told the listening men who he was and began to explain the nature of the voyage. "We shall travel to the famous Spice Islands," he said. "We shall travel by a new route, which will be faster and safer than any now known. We shall bring back fabulous cargoes of spices. Every man who travels with me will return to Seville a thousand times richer than he is now."

The Captain General paused. Something was wrong. The men were listening, but they looked at him with expressions of fear. The silence persisted. Finally one of the sailors, a leather-skinned man with one eye, spoke up. "We'll not sail with you. None of us."

"Why not?" asked Magellan.

The man squinted at Magellan with his good eye until it almost closed. "We've heard about where you're going to take us."

"What have you heard?"

The sailor opened his eye wide and stared at the Captain General. "You're going to take your ships into waters infested by devils."

"And sea monsters as big as three galleons," said another.

"Not true," Magellan began, but the men shouted him down. "We'll not sail with you . . . Devils . . . sea monsters . . ."

Magellan tried another tavern and got the same reception. And again, in a third and fourth. In the fifth tavern he learned who had been spreading the rumors—the clever Portuguese consul, Alvarez. He had done his job well. The superstitious seamen would have no part of Magellan or his expedition.

Magellan did not allow this to daunt him. He continued to talk to seamen in one tavern after another. He sought out merchants in the marketplace and asked them for the names of able-bodied men who might be enlisted for service aboard his ships. Eventually a crew was gathered, though it was not quite the kind Magellan had hoped for. They were an odd assortment—men of every race and country, among them thieves and murderers, desperate fugitives from justice willing to go anywhere to keep out of the hands of the law. The motley collection contained very few experienced sailors, but Magellan took comfort in the fact that among the skilled men most were Portuguese with whom he had sailed on earlier voyages.

This comfort was short-lived. Bishop Fonseca, who had been biding his time, watching the preparations carefully, now spoke to the king, telling him there were too many Portuguese on the expedition rolls, and that he was in danger of seeing his own ships delivered by the foreigners to King Manuel.

This time the Spanish king listened to Fonseca. He summoned Magellan and presented him with an order that there were to be no more than five Portuguese among the officers and crew. But again Magellan was able to assert his influence with the king. Though dismayed by the order, he managed to convince Charles to revise it and grant him the right to employ twenty-four Portuguese. Actually, by sailing time, there were thirty-seven men from Portugal aboard the five ships, among them Juan Serrano, Francisco's brother, who was to captain the *Santiago*. There were Spanish friends as well. Magellan found it reassuring that young Duarte Barbosa, his wife's cousin, would be included in the expedition.

In the end, nevertheless, Fonseca had his measure of success. Besides his nephew, Cartagena, who was to captain the *San Antonio,* the bishop was able to obtain jobs for two other captains loyal to him: Luis de Mendoza and Gaspar Quesada, who would command the *Victoria* and the *Concepcion,* respectively. Fonseca also placed his men in three other vital positions: chief pilot, expedition treasurer, and chief weapons officer.

At first Magellan did not understand the nature of the odds being set up against him. He proceeded as quickly as he could with the final business of supplying the vessels —a tremendous task. The ships were expected to be gone two years, perhaps three. All manner of equipment would be needed—blacksmithing tools for the repair of arms and weapons, mason's tools for building forts in the lands Magellan claimed for Spain, spare timbers for the ships, and carpenter's tools to shape them. Quantities of canvas were required, and medical supplies.

Goods for trading had to be purchased. In addition to bars of copper and iron, and bolts of cloth, there were fishhooks, mirrors, bells, colored crystals, and small knives, all articles which had proved valuable before in bartering with the natives of the East.

Special attention had to be paid to food. They could expect to take aboard fresh supplies from time to time where they landed, but no one knew how long the ships would be at sea, so a plentiful stock of rations had to be placed in the stores. Foods which could be kept for a long time without spoiling made up the bulk of the fare the men would eat: sailor's biscuit or hardtack, salted beef and pork, cheeses, dried and pickled fish. There were also great casks of water and wine.

Once more Sebastian Alvarez, the Portuguese consul, played a treacherous role. He bribed the harbor guards to look the other way, then had some of the food supplies stolen, knowing that men at sea without rations were likely to mutiny and force Magellan to return.

Alvarez was successful. At the time the fleet was ready to leave Seville, over half the food stocks were missing, and Magellan knew nothing of it.

Just before the ships sailed, a young man reported to Magellan. His name was Antonio Pigafetta; he was a member of a noble Italian family. King Charles sent word to Magellan asking, as a personal favor, that Pigafetta be allowed to accompany the expedition.

Magellan liked the young nobleman at once and placed him aboard his flagship, the *Trinidad*. It is history's good fortune that he did. Pigafetta kept a detailed diary. His lively, informative account has been preserved and is today our chief source of knowledge about the voyage.

In August, 1519, almost two years after Magellan received his appointment as Captain General, the fleet weighed anchor.

Seville is on a river, the Guadalquiver, about seventy-five miles from the sea. This turned out to be fortunate for Magellan, for while the ships were still moving down the river on the way to open water, the food shortages were discovered. The fleet dropped anchor again at San Lucar, a city at the mouth of the river. It took another month to replenish the stolen supplies.

Magellan's wife Beatriz journeyed to San Lucar, and they were able to spend a few more weeks together. But much as this aspect of the delay pleased him, Magellan could not relax. The voyage before him promised to be both arduous and rewarding. He longed to begin it.

The morning of September 20 was warm and crystal clear. A light breeze ruffled the surface of the river.

On the quarterdeck of the flagship, Magellan gave an order. The crew chanted a rhythmic song as they heaved at the lines and hauled canvas skyward. The breeze caught the white sails and filled them. Now the other four ships followed suit. Led by the *Trinidad,* the fleet moved majestically downriver, aided by the ebbing tide. Magellan felt the first surging ocean swell.

At long last they were under way.

Departure and a Plot

THE FIRST destination lay quite near: an island in the Canary group called Tenerife. It would take a week of sailing through well-charted waters to reach it. Magellan planned to use this leg of the voyage as a kind of shakedown for both ships and crews. Many of the men had never been to sea before. They had to become accustomed to hard work and severe discipline.

It was extremely important for the five ships to remain within sight of one another at all times. This was a simple enough task by day, but during the hours of darkness it could be a problem. They managed it by a kind of code routine. Magellan's flagship, the *Trinidad,* was to display a single lantern or a combination of lights which would tell the other ships exactly what their speed and course should be. At twilight, just before the lanterns were hoisted, each ship in turn was expected to sail close to the *Trinidad*. Each captain was required to salute Magellan with the words, "God save you, Sir Captain General and Master and good ship's company." They would then receive their instructions for the night watches.

Before very long this evening ritual, which was customary among all Spanish fleets, was to become a source of danger to Magellan. But during that first week the system worked well. The little armada skimmed along before perfect winds, and at the end of seven days the lookout on the flagship sighted the towering mountain peak which set Tenerife apart from the other Canary Islands.

They stayed several days on the island, taking on fresh water and additional supplies. The crew enjoyed their last leave ashore, but Magellan, ever impatient to press on, would have been happier if they had not stopped at Tenerife at all.

It was lucky they did. Shortly before they were due to sail from the island, a dispatch boat, a fast caravel which had raced all the way from Spain, swung into harbor. The captain carried with him a letter for Magellan.

The letter was from his father-in-law, Diogo Barbosa. "Beware, my son," it began. "The man we thought of as a friend, Bishop Fonseca, is in truth our enemy. He seeks to destroy you. Fonseca has informed the Portuguese of the course you intend to take across the Atlantic. He has urged them to attack your fleet, kill you, and place his own nephew, Juan de Cartagena, in command once you are dead. If for any reason this plan does not work, Cartagena has instructions to provoke a mutiny against you, and to take over command in this fashion. Beware, my son. Beware of the traitors in your midst."

Magellan was shocked. But he had complete trust in the word of his father-in-law. If Barbosa said Fonseca was an enemy, an enemy he was. Nor did Magellan doubt now that the proud Cartagena could turn against him.

He retired to the cabin of his flagship and thought about what he should do. He could, as Captain General, have Cartagena arrested and sail from Tenerife without him. But as yet the bishop's nephew had not questioned Magellan's authority. If Magellan made a move against him without having a very good reason, the rest of the Spanish captains, and the Spanish crews, would surely rebel, and no one could blame them.

No, he had to be more careful, and much more clever. He decided to act as if he knew nothing about the plot. He was certain that Cartagena would sooner or later show his hand. Magellan intended to make sure it was sooner, and to bring this about in such a way that he, not Cartagena, would end up in control of the situation. But it was not going to be easy.

The first problem was to avoid meeting the Portuguese armada which Barbosa had warned would be lying in wait. Magellan's planned course was southwest, designed to bring the ships to South America by the shortest route. Now, however, two days after leaving Tenerife, he ordered the course changed so that the fleet was sailing almost due south. Then he waited to see how Cartagena would react.

The bishop's nephew was also clever. He grumbled about the change in course, but he never allowed his objections to reach the point of open rebellion. The other two Spanish captains took their lead from Cartagena. They steered their ships south, following the *Trinidad*, but letting it be known as loudly as they dared that they thought Magellan was mad.

For a while fortune was with the Captain General. The winds were fair from the north, and for two weeks the ships made excellent headway.

Then, on the fourteenth day after Magellan had given the order to change course, clouds began forming overhead, rapidly growing darker and heavier, until it seemed to the men on the ships that they could reach out and touch the black billowing masses. There was scarcely time to shorten sail before the wind struck, shrieking through the rigging, making the ocean boil up, and sending gigantic waves smashing into the top-heavy galleons.

Even Magellan, in all his years at sea, had never witnessed such a storm. He must have felt fear, but he knew he could not show it. He stood erect on the quarterdeck, occasionally shouting encouragement to the crew of the *Trinidad*, peering through the pelting rain for a glimpse of his other ships.

Departure and a Plot

He saw them, wallowing like the *Trinidad,* rolling over so far that their shrouds were often under water.

Night fell. Lightning crackled. Thunder, louder than the roar of a hundred cannons, boomed from every quarter. The men were cowering on the deck, bawling with terror. But Magellan, as casually as if it were an ordinary evening, ordered the signal lanterns to be lighted and hoisted aloft.

His calmness steadied the crew. The ship was still rolling heavily, tossing on the wild waters, but somehow the men were not as frightened. Most of them were still praying, many of them moaning, desperately seasick, but now they felt they would survive. And shortly after midnight, one of the men shouted and pointed up at the

Magellan's vessels in stormy Atlantic waters

top of the *Trinidad's* mast, where a lovely blue and white light was flickering. It was St. Elmo's fire—a frequent enough phenomenon during thunderstorms which we know now to be caused by the buildup of electricity on some exposed object, but which to the crew of the *Trinidad* was an omen sent by God to tell them the storm would soon subside.

Then it was over. The rain stopped. The wind died down by morning. But—ominously—it died down completely, and showed no sign of rising again. The sea grew glassy. The ships lay becalmed under a brutal noonday sun.

A long afternoon waned. Night came, then dawn and another day. Surely a breeze would spring up, enough to give relief from the heat, if not to send the ships once more on their course.

But the second day passed without even a ripple stirring the smooth surface of the ocean. The ships stood silent in a strange shimmering haze which gave them the appearance of ghosts.

And ghosts they would most certainly be if soon there was not not enough wind to give them motion. The third day the water barrels burst from the heat, and what little water remained went bad. On the sixth day the sun melted the caulking out of the seams of three of the ships, and they began to leak badly. Still no wind. The tenth day Magellan learned that practically all their food was putrid and had to be thrown overboard.

It is remarkable that the men did not mutiny then.

Certainly there was talk of it, and one may be sure Cartagena and the other two Spanish captains made no effort to stop their crews from cursing the fool of a Portuguese who had brought them into a living hell. But Cartagena was not stupid enough to try taking over the fleet now. He did not know how much longer the calm would last. Until it was over, and they were under way again, he was content to wait and let Magellan take full blame for their plight.

The fifteenth day, and still no breeze. Magellan issued orders that the small supplies of food and water were to be rationed. Naturally, this did not make him any more popular with the men. Cartagena smiled and continued to bide his time, but even he must have wondered if the wind would ever blow again.

Finally, on the twenty-first day a breeze sprang up and filled the sails. The men shouted with relief. For the moment they forgot any thought of mutiny.

Not Cartagena. This, he thought, was the time to make his move.

The fleet was now sailing steadily westward. On the first evening after the wind returned, Magellan waited for each ship to come up alongside the *Trinidad* and for the captains to salute him as they had been instructed. His cousin Juan Serrano brought up the *Santiago*, repeated the greeting, "God save you, Sir Captain General and Master and good ship's company." Then came Quesada in the *Concepcion* and Mendoza in the *Victoria*.

They also repeated the prescribed words and received orders from Magellan for the night watch.

Suddenly the Captain General grew wary. Cartagena was taking his time bringing the *San Antonio* alongside, and when the galleon eventually drew within shouting distance, it was not Cartagena but the boatswain who hailed Magellan. "God save you," he called out, "Captain and Master."

Magellan called back, demanding that the proper greeting be presented and that Cartagena himself deliver it.

Juan de Cartagena came on deck and sauntered to the rail. The two ships lay close enough together for Magellan to see the insolent expression on the Spanish captain's face. "I sent the best man on my ship to greet you," Cartagena cried. "Perhaps next time I'll have my cabin boy do it."

Magellan stared at him. This was it, then, the act of rebellion he had been expecting. The men on both ships watched the Captain General, waiting for Magellan to explode into fury.

Nothing happened. Magellan continued to stare back at Cartagena without speaking a word. The Spanish captain sneered and ordered his ship to swing back into position.

For the next three nights Cartagena made no effort to come alongside the *Trinidad*. He had defied Magellan and won. Things were going more easily than he had hoped.

Departure and a Plot

On the fourth night Captain Mendoza reported that one of the officers aboard the *Victoria* had been caught stealing. Ordinarily, Magellan might have instructed Mendoza to punish the man himself. Now, however, he ordered the culprit to be brought aboard the flagship the next day and tried for his crime. All the captains were to come aboard as well and act as a court.

The time came; the captains arrived, Cartagena swaggering, sure of himself. The trial was held and sentence passed. Magellan thanked the captains and told them they were free to return to their ships.

They got up to leave, but Cartagena motioned them all to sit down again. He began to complain loudly about what he called Magellan's idiocy in having changed course after the fleet left Tenerife. If Magellan had been any kind of captain, Cartagena said, he would have held the original course, and the ships would not have been becalmed.

Magellan did not interrupt Cartagena, nor did he reply when the Spaniard finished speaking. He sat watching him as though nothing had been said.

Cartagena could not believe what was happening. Was Magellan this much of a coward? He got to his feet, shouting at the Captain General, "You are not fit to command! I for one refuse to follow another order you give!"

This was exactly what Magellan had been waiting for. He leaped out of his chair, seized the astounded Cartagena by the shirt, and cried out, "You are my prisoner!"

Cartagena tried to struggle, but Magellan held him fast. An instant later the door burst open, and the captain of the guard strode in, followed by several soldiers. "You heard him?" asked Magellan. "You heard him speak words of mutiny?"

"I heard him," said the captain of the guard.

Magellan handed the rebel over to the soldiers with instructions that Cartagena be placed in irons.

Only now did the other two Spanish captains come to life. No doubt they had been aware of what Cartagena intended to do, but Magellan had acted so rapidly they scarcely understood what had taken place. Now they pleaded with Magellan not to put Cartagena in irons. Captain Mendoza said he would take him aboard the *Victoria* and would be responsible for him.

Magellan hesitated. A long voyage still lay ahead of them. Mendoza and Quesada were skilled captains. Even if Magellan could not trust them, he still needed them. He gave his consent, and Mendoza took Cartagena back to the *Victoria*.

Magellan then appointed a new captain, Antonio de Coca, to take command of the *San Antonio*. That evening Coca brought his ship alongside and greeted Magellan in the required manner.

Cartagena's mutiny had failed.

Two weeks later the coast of Brazil was sighted, and a few days after that the fleet sailed into the bay at what is now known as Rio de Janeiro.

Rio was then, as it is today, a beautiful harbor. Every

The arrival in Rio

man aboard the five ships, Magellan included, looked toward the green shoreline, thankful that the first part of the voyage was over, hoping they might find here a few blessed days of peace.

They did indeed find peace in Rio, but it was the last they would have for many months. For some among them the days in Rio were to be the last moments of peace they would find on earth.

Winter Haven

THE DAYS in Rio were sunlit and mellow, the nights balmy and free of care. The natives of the beautiful bay were friendly and eager to trade. Once again the sailors had fresh food. Antonio Pigafetta, the young Italian nobleman who was writing down a careful account of the voyage, was amazed at how cheaply food could be bought; a few beads or a brass bell would secure great quantities of fish and meat. Pigafetta himself traded a playing card for six chickens.

Life in Rio was sweet, too sweet. The men wanted to remain there and grumbled audibly when Magellan set the date for their departure.

Nor was their stay entirely free of trouble. Antonio de Coca, whom Magellan had placed in command of Cartagena's ship after he had imprisoned the rebel, began to hatch a desperate plot of his own. Coca was a cousin to Cartagena, and now he wanted to release his relative and help him seize control of the fleet.

Magellan discovered the plot in time. He was extremely lenient with Coca. Although he could have had him executed, he merely dismissed him from his captaincy and appointed another man, Alvaro de Mesquita, to command the *San Antonio.*

On December 27, 1519—a midsummer day in the southern hemisphere—Magellan assembled his men and ships, sailed out of Rio bay, and set a course to the south. The fleet stayed close to the coast, never out of sight of land. Magellan did not want to chance missing the entrance to the *paso.*

Each evening, after figuring out the position of the armada of ships, Magellan retired to his cabin and checked his calculations against the map he had discovered three years before in the chartroom at Lisbon. Everything was going well. Soon they would reach the entrance to the passage. Then they would turn westward, navigate the strait, and in a matter of weeks they would find themselves in the rich Moluccas. Magellan was already thinking of the pleasant reunion he would have with his old companion Francisco Serrano. Now at last he could allow himself to picture a triumphant return to Spain, his ships laden with the wealth of the East.

On January 11, the lookout on the flagship sighted three mountains rising from a huge cape projecting out into the sea. As the fleet rounded the point of land,

Magellan became jubilant. There, exactly as it was shown on his secret map, lay a great broad inlet, stretching westward as far as one could see.

This, then, must be the *paso*.

The morale of the men, which had been growing steadily worse since the departure from Rio, began to pick up. There was general rejoicing, and even the Spanish captains became cheerful, mingling with their crews and talking enthusiastically of what they would do with their immense wealth when they returned to Spain. Laughter and songs rang out across the water as the five ships dropped anchor in the shelter of the headland.

Magellan decided not to sail westward with the entire

A sixteenth-century galleon. The figure at left is using a sextant to check the ship's position.

fleet at once. Better to send the lightest vessel on an exploratory journey so they would know what lay ahead.

The Captain General called Juan Serrano to his cabin. "You will sail the *Santiago* into the strait," Magellan instructed his cousin. "It will not be necessary at the moment to take detailed soundings. The main thing we are interested in is finding out whether the water is deep enough for the heavier ships."

"How far into the strait shall I go?" Serrano asked.

"A total distance of 150 miles. If by then you have not emerged into open ocean, return and make your report." Then, remembering the account of Juan de Solis' death at the hands of hostile natives, Magellan added, "You will note the nature of the coast, but under no circumstances are you to land." He smiled at Serrano. "Good luck, cousin."

Serrano saluted and left the cabin.

Magellan counted on Serrano's being gone about three weeks, perhaps even a month. While the *Santiago* was away, the Captain General kept the other ships busy charting the mouth of the inlet; each evening, though, they returned to the fleet anchorage.

Not quite two weeks after Serrano left, Magellan saw the *Santiago* on the horizon, speeding toward the armada. The little ship's early return could mean just one thing: the *paso* was short, much shorter than the map showed it to be. Magellan's spirits soared. Through the few miles of the passage, then a brief trip across the gentle western sea, and—

Suddenly he noticed that the *Santiago* was not flying any pennants from her masthead. Probably in his excitement Serrano had forgotten to order the raising of the celebration signals. Magellan would pretend to be angry about this. That night, when the captains were drinking toasts with the special wine set aside for this great event, Magellan would make a joke about Serrano's forgetfulness. It did not really matter. They had found the *paso*. That was all that counted.

The *Santiago* drew closer. Magellan could hardly wait for Serrano to hail him and shout the good news.

Then, as the tiny ship came about and maneuvered toward its anchorage, the Captain General's heart sank. Serrano was standing on the quarterdeck, looking in Magellan's direction. But his expression was unsmiling, his shoulders bowed.

Moments later, Magellan learned the reason for his cousin's dejection. "We sailed westward, according to your orders," Serrano said. "For the first few days of the journey everything went well. The passage was broad, so broad that we couldn't see a shoreline on either side. Then—" He paused, looking at Magellan. "Then, after about a week, we entered a much narrower channel. This did not trouble me—"

"But something else did."

Serrano nodded. "I began to notice that the outgoing tide seemed much stronger than the incoming. At first I wondered—perhaps this more powerful tide could be coming from the western ocean we were seeking. But somehow—well, it simply didn't behave the way a tide should. I decided to find out. I ordered a bucket lowered over the side and filled with water. My men brought the bucket back up to the deck—" Serrano turned away. He was almost mumbling now. "I tasted the water. It was not salty, the way sea water should be. It was fresh and sweet."

Magellan stared at Serrano. The meaning of his cousin's words was perfectly clear. The channel he had been following was not the *paso* at all, but a large river.

Magellan received the news in silence. It was a bitter disappointment. All his hopes and plans had centered about finding the passage at precisely this latitude; the secret map had led him astray. The dreams, the struggles, the months and years of waiting, everything had come to nothing in a single moment of failure.

Was there indeed a *paso*? Magellan felt there had to be, to the south. But no one had yet explored the seas farther south. Perhaps there would be only unending coastline and steadily worsening weather. It was February now, autumn in this part of the world. Already on the trip from Rio they had run into some moderately fierce storms. With winter approaching, could he dare take his tiny armada into an ocean where gales might howl everlastingly, where fear of the unknown might turn his crews into shrieking, helpless madmen?

Word of Serrano's discoverey spread quickly through the fleet. The Spanish captains once more began to grumble against Magellan. They had known all along, they said, that the Captain General was a fraud. The sailors looked hopefully toward the flagship. Now that it was certain that the *paso* did not exist, surely Magellan would take them back to Rio, where they would spend the winter, and then return to Spain.

The day after Serrano's return, Magellan stood on the *Trinidad's* quarterdeck gazing westward, toward what he had believed to be the route to the Moluccas. Then he swung around and directed a somber stare at the open ocean. The decision he knew he must make was shaping in his mind.

He could not bring himself to believe the *paso* did not exist. There *must* be an exit to the western ocean; and surely it could not lie much farther south. They had come this far. They would press on.

Magellan gave the order to sail southward. The captains and their crews heard it in angry silence, but they obeyed.

Almost at once the sea fought them. The weather turned bitter cold. Hurricane-force winds shredded the rigging, tore at the masts. Mountainous waves crashed over the five frail ships; the waves encountered off the African coast seemed like millpond ripples in comparison. Salt spray stung the faces and hands of the men, freezing on their clothing. The decks became treacherous ice runs. Some of the sailors were swept overboard by the monstrous seas. Often one or another of the ships came close to foundering.

Still they continued to make their painful way southward. They ventured fearfully yet hopefully into each bay which looked as if it might be the passage they sought. Then, discouraged when they found it was not, they crept out again onto open ocean to struggle once more with the angry waters.

Finally, on the last day of March, having voyaged a full thousand miles south of the false *paso*, they sighted a tiny bay. There could be no thought that this one was the passage. Even a mile out from the entrance, the end of the bay could be clearly seen—a crescent-shaped shore lying bleak and gloomy beneath heavy clouds. But at least it appeared to be sheltered from the bitter wind.

Magellan's flagship entered the bay, followed by the other four vessels. The bottom of the bay was firm, suitable for anchorage. The Captain General sent out a landing party. There seemed to be an abundance of fish, water birds, and firewood about.

They had come a long way. No one knew how much farther they had to go. Magellan considered, then issued an order. They would spend the rest of the winter here. He named the bay Port San Julian.

He might as well have named it Port Despair.

9

The Second Mutiny

EVEN HAD EVERYTHING been going perfectly well all along, Magellan could have expected trouble. The officers and men of his expedition had sailed from Spain believing that, after a short voyage across the Atlantic and through a passage to the west, they would soon find themselves in the fabulous Moluccas.

Instead, many months after they had set out, they were cooped up in a barren bay which boasted few comforts and fewer prospects of comfort to come. They saw themselves commanded by a man many of them considered mad and some considered evil. They could neither understand nor sympathize with Magellan's insistence on searching for a *paso* they had long since decided did not even exist. Why, they asked, when they might have turned back and even now be home in Spain, or at least in Rio, were they continuing to stay on in this dreary, frigid land? Truly, no one could blame them for being discontented.

Of all the men on the five ships, probably only four were unquestioningly loyal to Magellan: his slave Enrique, his cousin Juan Serrano, Duarte Barbosa, and the young Italian, Pigafetta. But a fifth man was beginning to admire the stern Captain General. His name was Espinosa, and he was captain of the guard aboard the *Trinidad*. His growing affection for Magellan was to prove highly valuable in the events which followed the anchoring in Port San Julian.

Magellan could count on Serrano, but his cousin commanded the *Santiago*, smallest of the ships. He knew that Mesquita, whom he had placed in charge of the *San Antonio*, was not the brightest or most capable of men, but Magellan was sure he would at least obey orders.

Ranged against him—men he was certain would attack him at the first opportunity—were Quesada on the *Concepcion* and Mendoza on the *Victoria*. Not to be dismissed from consideration, though he was technically a prisoner aboard the *Concepcion*, was the mastermind behind all plots against Magellan, Juan de Cartagena.

Danger undoubtedly lay ahead. Still, Magellan controlled three ships to the Spanish captains' two. He could not hope for a completely peaceful winter, but he felt it might at least be possible to keep the discontented officers from stirring the expedition to open rebellion.

This hope was destroyed the very first night in San Julian.

The flaw lay in the fact that Mesquita did *not* obey orders. He failed to post a guard aboard his ship. Shortly after midnight, Captain Quesada, accompanied by thirty armed men, lowered a boat from the *Concepcion*, rowed stealthily across the dark surface of the bay, and crept aboard the *San Antonio*. No one challenged them as they made their way to the captain's cabin. There they found Mesquita, and before he understood what was going on, the rebels seized and bound him. Mesquita's master-at-arms happened to pass his captain's cabin at just this moment. He made an effort to stop the invaders, but his heroism was futile. They killed him. They then spread out through the ship. There was no further resistance, and moments later they were in control of the *San Antonio*.

Magellan knew nothing of this until late the next morning. Then the longboat from the flagship, making the rounds of the other vessels to pick up men for a wood-gathering detail ashore, was roughly turned away from the *San Antonio*. It continued to the *Victoria* and the *Concepcion*. At each of these ships the men in the longboat were told to keep away, that the ships were now in control of crews who no longer took orders from Magellan.

The balance of power had shifted overnight. The *Trinidad* and the little *Santiago* stood alone against the other three ships.

The Second Mutiny

Magellan considered his situation carefully. His only chance for victory over the mutineers lay in guessing what their next move would be, and then taking steps to outmaneuver them.

He reasoned that Cartagena would, as usual, be the chief plotter in the revolt. Cartagena wanted one thing above all others: Magellan's death. He might try ordering the three rebel ships to bear down on the *Trinidad*, rake it with cannon fire until it was helpless, then send a boarding party onto the flagship to murder Magellan.

Cartagena might try this. He was desperate enough. But Magellan was relying on something else he was sure lay in Cartagena's mind. The *Trinidad* was the property of King Charles. If Cartagena sank her, or even damaged her beyond repair, he would certainly have to defend himself before a court of inquiry when he returned to Spain. There would be witnesses. Cartagena could not be sure of the story they would tell. If, in his attack on the *Trinidad*, his cannon fire killed even one innocent man, this could prove embarrassing for both Cartagena and his uncle, Bishop Fonseca.

Therefore, Magellan thought, Cartagena would resort to some type of trickery, the exact nature of which Magellan as yet had no way of knowing.

He did not have to wait long. From noon on, for over two hours, boats scuttled back and forth between the three rebel ships. Magellan stood on the quarterdeck of the *Trinidad* and carefully observed this flurry of activity.

Then, at midafternoon, everything suddenly became quiet. The three ships lay motionless, not a single crew member visible on their decks.

Magellan continued his vigil. He ordered Espinosa, his captain of the guard, to be ready in case the ships did actually begin to move toward the *Trinidad*.

Another hour passed. Suddenly the deck of the *San Antonio* came alive with men milling about and calling to one another. Magellan tensed, watching, but the other two ships remained quiet, and eventually the excitement on the *San Antonio* subsided.

Not entirely, though. A longboat was being briskly lowered into the water. A crew was sent over the side to man it, and in a few moments the boat was speeding across the water toward the *Trinidad*. As it drew closer Magellan noticed that the small craft contained six enlisted men, but not a single officer.

This was undoubtedly Cartagena's opening ploy in some complicated game of treachery. What did he have in mind?

The crew of the longboat secured their craft to the side of the *Trinidad* and came aboard. Magellan limped forward to meet them. One of the men handed him a letter. Magellan glanced at it, saw that it was signed not by Cartagena but by Gaspar Quesada, who had taken over the *San Antonio*.

The letter was far from hostile in tone. It said that King Charles had placed Magellan in charge of the armada, and no one intended to dispute his right to command. However, differences had arisen between himself and his senior officers, as Magellan must freely admit. The captains of the rebel ships wished to discuss these differences. Would the Captain General therefore be generous enough to allow himself to be rowed back to the *San Antonio*, where, by friendly talk, all the points of conflict could be cleared up? The Captain General had their assurance as officers and gentlemen that he would be completely safe.

Magellan thought quickly. He knew the mutineers did not for one instant expect him to return with the longboat. More likely they merely wished to make this letter part of the record. Mutiny was a serious crime. Cartagena could say later that he had tried in every reasonable way to discuss matters with Magellan. He would be able to add that Magellan had refused his offer.

Perhaps later in the day there would be a less friendly note, larded with insults. Perhaps Cartagena counted on provoking the Captain General's stormy temper. If he could goad Magellan into firing on the rebel ships—

Whatever Cartagena's strategy, Magellan had no intention of falling in with it, or even of waiting to see what the rebels' next step would be.

He had dreamed too long. He had come too far. There might not be a passage to the Moluccas, but if there was, Magellan intended to find it. He could not do this alone. He needed all his ships, and he needed the crews who manned them. The mutiny must be crushed, promptly, before it infected even the men aboard the two loyal ships.

Magellan paced the quarterdeck, pretending to think. Actually he was all the while edging closer to Espinosa. He whispered a few words to him, and a moment later the captain of the guard called out a quiet command. His soldiers stepped forward, seized the six men from the *San Antonio*, and hustled them below deck. So swiftly and efficiently was this done that no one on any of the other ships knew what was happening.

So far so good. Magellan was playing a desperate game, one which depended on precise timing. It was a gamble, but unless he made the attempt, he would certainly lose everything.

He went below and directed Espinosa and five of his soldiers to change clothes with the men from the *San Antonio*. He then drew the captain of the guard aside and issued further instructions.

A short time later Espinosa and his five companions lowered themselves into the longboat. But instead of steering for the *San Antonio*, they rowed straight to the *Victoria*. Their disguises prevented the men on the rebel ships from becoming suspicious.

They climbed aboard, asked for the captain. Mendoza naturally recognized Espinosa, but evidently it did not occur to him to wonder what the captain of the *Trinidad*'s guard was doing in the *San Antonio*'s longboat. He did not need to worry about six lightly armed men, not when he stood firmly on the deck of a ship he commanded, surrounded by his own soldiers.

Espinosa handed the rebel captain a note from Magellan. It was brief, asking only that Mendoza return with Espinosa to the *Trinidad*.

Mendoza laughed and began a scornful reply. He never finished it. Espinoza seized him and thrust a dagger through his throat. Mendoza died immediately.

The *Victoria*'s soldiers stared unbelievingly, then leaped forward. Magellan had banked on their entire attention being concentrated on Mendoza and Espinosa. At just the proper moment he had sent off the *Trinidad*'s longboat, crammed with soldiers, who now swarmed aboard the *Victoria*.

Taken by surprise, their captain dead, the *Victoria*'s crew surrendered at once. Strangely enough, the maneuver had so far attracted only mild attention from the other rebel ships, but Espinosa knew that time was precious. He quickly gave the order to raise anchors and set sail. Silently, swiftly, the *Victoria* swung past her sister ships, across the bay to the mouth of the harbor, where she took up a position beside the *Trinidad* and the *Santiago*.

Only now did Cartagena, summoned by his men to the deck of the *Concepcion*, realize that his own trickery had been flung back in his face. Three ships again faced his two. Magellan had won.

The very next day the Captain General held a court martial. Mendoza's body was propped up at the trial, and a solemn verdict of guilty was pronounced against the dead man. Captain Quesada and his servant, who had murdered the master-at-arms of the *San Antonio*, were both sentenced to death. But no one could be found to execute them. Finally the servant was offered a pardon if he would carry out the sentence against Quesada. It was a cruel choice, almost an impossible one, but the servant's desire to live was stronger than his loyalty. He accepted the pardon and beheaded his master, Quesada.

Magellan would have liked to be rid of Cartagena as well. But the Bishop's nephew had been clever enough to remain behind the scenes during the uprising. Although Magellan knew that Cartagena had planned the mutiny, he could not prove it. There were no grounds for condemning the Spanish nobleman to death. Magellan would have to think carefully about how to deal with Cartagena.

10

The Fleet Moves On

THE REBELLION was over, but other serious problems faced the Captain General. Food was growing scarce. True, there was still enough fresh meat and fish, but they would last only as long as the ships remained in port. The supplies of biscuit and wine, which were intended to feed them if and when they crossed the western ocean, were becoming dangerously low. Magellan had already cut the ration once; he was unwilling to order another reduction so soon after the mutiny.

There was only one answer. They could not afford to remain in San Julian until spring. Now, even while the winter gales were still shrieking outside the bay, they would have to sail southward.

Once again the *Santiago*, because of its shallow draft, would press ahead and explore the unknown waters.

Serrano prepared his ship for the voyage, but before he could sail, a particularly ferocious storm swept down on them, delaying the *Santiago*'s departure. On the next day, the lookout of Serrano's ship, who was maintaining a constant watch on the open sea, waiting for the storm to abate, happened to glance toward the shore. What he saw filled him with excitement and fear.

A man dressed in animal skins was walking over the crest of the hill down to the shore of the bay. Others on the ship, alerted by the lookout's cry, gazed toward the shore. They could scarcely believe their eyes. The man was well over eight feet tall.

Nor did their surprise end when Magellan went ashore at the head of a cautious landing party. The native turned out to be friendly enough, but his appetite proved to be

A Patagonian native such as the ones Magellan saw, as drawn by a sixteenth-century observer

as enormous and outlandish as his size. Pigafetta describes how he downed a bucket of water in what appeared to be a single swallow. Somehow, Pigafetta does not say exactly how or why, the stranger was given a few rats, which he proceeded to eat alive. After receiving some beads and bells the man went away, but next day he was back again with several companions, men and women, all as huge as he. Magellan gave them the name of Patagonians, which means "big feet"; a large section of Argentina today is still called Patagonia, after these early inhabitants.

The storm died on the third day. The monstrous waves outside the harbor subsided, and the sea resumed its customary long black swell. Serrano set out.

He sailed the *Santiago* southward for more than two weeks. Other storms rose, holding down his progress most days to a meager four or five miles.

Serrano was just about to turn back when he sighted the mouth of a large river which he named the Santa Cruz. He explored a short distance upstream and found an excellent harbor, considerably better than San Julian. He decided that on his return to the expedition's camp he would suggest to Magellan that winter quarters be transferred here.

Then bad luck struck again. Serrano had scarcely reached open water when a vicious squall sprang up. A particularly large wave smashed the *Santiago*'s rudder, leaving it nearly helpless. The ship with all its hands might have been lost at once had it not been for Serrano's skill as a captain. Steering only with sail, he brought the vessel close to shore, maneuvered it deftly through the pounding breakers, and managed to beach it without capsizing.

But the danger was not over. Waves still tore at the *Santiago*, and at any moment she could be swept back out to sea. Serrano ordered his men to assemble on the foredeck and to leap ashore one by one. One man, Serrano's Negro slave, lost his life in the process. He miscalculated the speed of an incoming wave, jumped at the wrong instant, and disappeared beneath the foaming waters.

The other thirty-seven men got safely ashore, but not a moment too soon. Just as Serrano himself abandoned ship, a gigantic comber bore down on the *Santiago* and plucked it off the beach as if it were a tiny bit of driftwood.

The crew was in a terrible predicament, shipwrecked on a barren shore with only the clothes on their backs, their chances of being rescued slim. But Serrano remained calm. He knew if he could only get word to Magellan, help would soon arrive. He sent two of his men overland, northward to San Julian. If they did not return within a reasonable length of time, he would send two more, and if necessary another two.

The journey by foot from Santa Cruz to San Julian was a nightmare. The two messengers tried to stay close to the shore, but they encountered great forbidding swamps which forced them to detour far inland. Winter winds froze them day and night. They saw a number of small animals and birds but had no way of capturing them, so their only food was roots and grass.

At length, nearly dead from starvation and cold, they stumbled across the last hill and down to the shore of San Julian Bay. They were so thin, so filthy, so covered with cuts and sores that Magellan and his men were at first unable to recognize them.

They told the Captain General their story, and he at once sent a rescue ship to pick up the castaways. He was of course relieved that practically all of the crew of the *Santiago* were still alive, but the loss of the little ship, which Magellan had counted on continuing to use for exploration, was a bitter blow.

When Serrano returned to San Julian he conferred with Magellan, who agreed with his cousin's recommendation. They would move to Santa Cruz for the rest of the winter.

But before they did, there was a difficult decision to make.

Magellan had hoped that the death of Mendoza and the execution of Quesada would mark the end of any mutinous activity. He hoped that Cartagena had learned a lesson, and would not make any further attempts to stir the men to revolt.

Cartagena did not learn. He still seemed unable to accept Magellan's authority. He began plotting another

*An artist's conception of the imprisonment of Cartagena
shows him placed in stocks.*

mutiny. Magellan learned about it and at once had the young nobleman placed under guard.

Now that the armada was leaving San Julian, the Captain General had to make up his mind how to punish Cartagena for his treachery. He knew that as long as the bishop's nephew was part of the expedition, there would be trouble. Yet Magellan was still not ready to execute him.

The morning of the fleet's departure Magellan announced his decision. Juan de Cartagena and a priest who had also been active in the last attempted mutiny were to be left behind on the shore of the bleak bay. They would not starve. Food was plentiful enough. But many years would probably pass before another ship would visit these waters.

In many ways the punishment was more severe than if the men had been sentenced to death. Half a century later another explorer, Sir Francis Drake, also wintered at San Julian. He too had to put down a mutiny, and he gave the leader of the revolt his choice of death or being left ashore. Drake's captain chose to die immediately rather than endure the torture of being marooned.

The four ships were now ready to leave San Julian. Magellan, of course, still commanded the *Trinidad.* Serrano took over the *Concepcion,* and Duarte Barbosa the *Victoria.* This left the *San Antonio.* Captain Mesquita was not a strong man, but he was an experienced officer, and Magellan decided to restore him to the command of the San Antonio. Mesquita's pilot was a clever navigator, Estevan Gomez, and Magellan felt that these two men between them could handle the fourth ship.

As the fleet filed slowly through the narrow mouth of the bay, Cartagena and the priest stood on the shore and watched them leave. The men aboard the ships looked back silently as the two figures grew smaller and smaller and eventually vanished behind the headland masking the harbor's entrance.

Then the fury of the ocean caught the ships. Howling winds and angry waters allowed no one time to think of Cartagena and his companion.

A few days later they reached Santa Cruz. It was late August. The southern winter was nearly over.

Magellan was still convinced that the *paso* existed. Though he had no idea exactly how and where he might find it, he was certain that he would.

And at least, with Cartagena gone, he was sailing with a company of men who would remain loyal to him no matter what happened.

Or so Magellan thought.

The Discovery

SANTA CRUZ was considerably more comfortable than cheerless San Julian. Magellan's men felt their spirits lifted. Magellan himself would have liked to sail on in his quest for the strait, even before spring, but he did not feel he could ask the crews to brave more of the everlasting winter storms. At the first sign of improvement in the weather they would leave. Meantime they would rest.

The trouble with rest is that it often means idleness. Aside from the gathering of firewood and the fetching of fresh water for drinking and cooking, there was little to keep the men busy. And idleness, when it continues too long, usually breeds discontent.

This time the man who provoked discord was not one

of the senior officers. Gomez, pilot of the *San Antonio*, gathered the captains together in a secret meeting. In the beginning he did not suggest mutiny, and this was what made his talk so dangerous.

Santa Cruz lay on a latitude of 50 degrees south. If the fleet sailed due east, the course would take them well below the tip of Africa. "From there," Gomez told the captains, "we could proceed without difficulty to the Moluccas by a route we all know." He looked at each of them in turn, then continued. "Would this not be more sensible than seeking some passage that no one, including Magellan, really knows anything about? A two-month voyage, most of it through warm and pleasant seas, would bring us to the rich Orient. Why should we go on with something which might not succeed, which might in fact leave us as poor as we are now?" He lowered his voice. "If we go on, who knows what will happen? We could all die. It would be so much simpler and wiser to sail in the other direction, and be certain of success."

It was a tempting proposal. Even Juan Serrano and Duarte Barbosa, both fiercely loyal to Magellan, found themselves considering it seriously.

Then Gomez made a grave error. When he saw that the captains were ready to go along with his plan, he grew overconfident. "There is one thing we must do," he said. "Before we sail eastward, we should return to San Julian and pick up Juan de Cartagena."

"Why?" Serrano asked.

The Discovery

Gomez looked at him with a bland smile. "Magellan is a madman," he said. "We all know it well by now. We should imprison Magellan and place Cartagena in command."

This brought Serrano and Barbosa to their senses. They turned on Gomez. "You are the one who is mad," Barbosa said. "We shall have no part of this nonsense."

Gomez realized he had gone too far. He soothed the two captains and succeeded in getting them to agree to at least ask Magellan for a conference. "We do have a right," he said, "to know what the Captain General's plans are. It can do no harm to suggest to him my idea of going to the Moluccas by way of Africa. But," he added hastily, "whatever the Captain General finally orders, we shall all accept."

The meeting was held in the Captain General's cabin. Magellan limped back and forth across the little room, saying nothing, while each captain spoke in turn.

When they had finished, they waited fearfully for the outburst. None came. Instead, Magellan agreed quietly that there was much merit in what they said. "I am as anxious as any of you to reach the Moluccas," he continued. "However, the charter I have received from King Charles states that I am to seek a new passage to the western ocean. I am duty-bound to do everything I can to find it." But then, for the first time, Magellan admitted openly that he was no longer sure of the location of the *paso*, nor in fact if it existed at all. "In view of this," he said, "I shall make you a slightly different proposal. If you will consent to continue southward, and if we do not discover the *paso* by the time we reach the seventy-fifth parallel, I myself will give the order to turn eastward and go to the Orient by way of Africa."

It seemed a fair enough bargain. The captains accepted it in good spirit. They even suggested sailing sooner than had been planned. No one thought Magellan would find the *paso*. The quicker they completed the search, the quicker they could head for familiar sea lanes, and then on to the Spice Islands.

In mid-October the fleet once more weighed anchor and sailed southward, ever deeper into unknown waters. The weather was improving. A breath of spring was in the air.

A few days of uneventful voyaging brought them to a large point of land jutting far out into the water. They rounded it and saw a broad bay. Far in the distance were snow-peaked mountains. The ships dropped anchor.

The point of land was like a hundred they had seen before, the bay like several dozens they had explored during the past six months. It was certain to be closed off by land, or else turn out to be the mouth of another river.

Magellan ordered the *Concepcion* and the *San Antonio* to sail farther up the bay and bring back a report. Captain Mesquita objected. "Sir, surely this is not the passage we

are looking for." He pointed to the west. "You can see
the end of the bay from here. Our supplies are low, sir.
Sailing farther into this inlet would be a waste of time.
I beg you, Sir Captain General, sail southward. Sail southward and get the search over with. Then we can turn to
the east."

Serrano was not so outspoken, though he too was not
very happy about making this exploration. But Magellan
insisted, and the two ships started out. The Captain
General stood on the deck of the *Trinidad*, watching
them leave.

They were still in sight when a sudden squall sprang
up, much like the one which had wrecked the *Santiago*
at Santa Cruz. Gusts of wind drove the two ships rapidly
westward, even as they were shortening sail. Magellan
saw them disappear in what seemed to be a tiny dead-end
inlet. The squall became a storm. Darkness fell. A full-
fledged gale was blowing now. Magellan went below and
sat gloomily in his cabin. He was certain the two ships
were lost, and with them his hopes for realizing his
dream.

The storm continued for several days. When it finally
subsided, Magellan prepared to make a search of the
shores of the bay. If the ships were lost, perhaps a few
of the men had survived. He would pick them up and
return to Spain. At this moment he did not even have
the heart to consider the alternate plan of sailing eastward to the Moluccas.

The *Trinidad's* lookout called down from the forward masthead. "Sir Captain General, smoke to the west."

Magellan nodded glumly. Then the ships *had* foundered. The smoke was undoubtedly coming from the signal fires of the men who had escaped drowning.

He heard the lookout calling again. Was the man out of his mind? "A sail!" he was shouting. Then, "Two ships! Two ships approaching!"

It was true. The *Concepcion* and the *San Antonio* were rounding the point at the far end of the bay, emerging from the same inlet where they had disappeared several days before. Smoke was indeed rising from each vessel, but now Magellan realized that it was coming from the ships' cannons. He could hear the sound now, the dull booming of salvo after salvo echoing across the tranquil water.

Magellan tried to control his elation. So many months of false hope, so many disappointments—he made himself wait quietly.

Then Serrano came aboard the flagship, bursting with excitement. He stood stiffly at attention as he delivered his report. "When our two ships were driven westward by the storm," he said, "we were sure nothing could save us from being wrecked. All we could see ahead was a rocky shore. The spray was flying high in the air from enormous waves battering the cliffs."

But just when it seemed that the ships would splinter themselves against the cliffs, Serrano had spied a tiny opening in the rock wall. It was a chance. The passage might lead nowhere, and the ships would still be smashed, but it was a chance they had had to take.

Serrano signaled to Mesquita, who had also seen the opening, and with great difficulty they turned their clumsy galleons broadside to the wind, then sent them wallowing through the channel.

"To our amazement," Serrano continued, "instead of the dead end we expected, we found ourselves emerging into another body of water, much more sheltered than the one we had left. We went through a second narrows and discovered a third and still quieter bay. Surely, we thought, this must be the end of it."

But no, there were other narrows and other bays. As they had forged ahead, Serrano noticed distinct evidence of a regularly rising and falling tide. Remembering his experience at the first inlet they had explored, after Rio, he lowered a bucket over the side of his ship. The water he brought up to the deck tasted salty. "I knew then it was no river," he said.

Magellan, who had been listening intently to his cousin's account, took a deep breath and let it out slowly. Only now did he allow himself to believe the news.

The *paso*—they had found the *paso*!

Magellan could not afford to waste time celebrating. He shouted an order. Chains clattered as the heavy anchors were weighed. Canvas snapped in the brisk wind. The sails were set, and the four ships began their westward journey.

Entering the paso

They passed the farthest point explored by Serrano and Mesquita. Bay after bay opened before them, strangely quiet stretches of water made more ghostly by the huge ice-capped mountains towering on either side.

No human beings were visible on the shore during

the day. But each night the men on the ships could see lights flickering deep in the valleys which wound upward from the water's edge. Because of these mysterious lights, Magellan named the region Tierra del Fuego, Land of Fire. (Later explorers learned that there were people on these shores but that they were terrified of strangers. Since Magellan and his men were the first outsiders these natives had ever seen, they kept themselves well concealed, never venturing out of their huts while the ships were in sight. The lights Magellan noticed were indeed fires. The people kept them burning constantly in their huts because they had not yet learned how to start a fire with flint or sticks or by using the rays of the sun. Just an ocean's span away from the bustling, cultivated society of Europe was a land still living in the Stone Age.)

After a number of days the fleet reached a place where the channel branched into two equally large arms. There was no way of knowing which was the better. Perhaps both would lead them to the sea. Perhaps—and this was a thought Magellan did not let himself dwell on—neither would be passable.

Rather than have all four ships explore each passage, Magellan decided to save time by dividing the armada. The *Concepcion* and the *San Antonio* would travel along the left-hand fork. A boat from the flagship under the command of Espinosa, Magellan's captain of the guard, was sent out in the other direction. The *Trinidad* and the *Victoria* remained at the point where the channel split.

It was understood that the two exploring ships and the boat were to return in no more than five days' time.

Four days later Espinosa was back, jubilant. His boat had reached open ocean. The passage from one sea to another was now an established fact.

When he heard the news, Magellan fell to his knees and wept with joy. His crew, who knew him only as a silent, somber man, must have marveled at the sight.

The Discovery

The next morning the *Concepcion* returned—alone. The channel they had traveled ended in rock-strewn narrows, quite unsuitable for safe navigation.

Serrano was surprised not to see the *San Antonio*. Two nights before, the pair of ships had dropped anchor fairly close together. At dawn, the *San Antonio* was gone. Serrano had assumed that Mesquita, for one reason or another, had decided to return before him.

Magellan directing the exploration of the paso *from a longboat*

*Magellan's route is shown on a sixteenth-century map of the
New World. At bottom is the* paso, *renamed for its dis-
coverer the* Strait of Magellan *(Fretum Magaliani).*

At first Magellan thought that the *San Antonio* might
have encountered trouble, perhaps even have been
wrecked. He sent scouting parties out to search for the
vessel. The patrols straggled back to base without any of
them having seen a sign of the missing ship.

It was Serrano who made another, more sinister, suggestion. He knew that Gomez, not Mesquita, was the real
commander of the ship. He also knew that Gomez had
been complaining about the sad state of the expedition's
supplies and had felt for some time that they should not
set out across another uncharted ocean without an

adequate supply of food on hand. Serrano's guess was that Gomez had either persuaded or forced Mesquita to desert the fleet and turn the *San Antonio* back toward Spain. They must have slipped by unseen in the night.

This guess was later proved to be correct. At the moment no one knew what had happened. All that seemed important was that one of the armada's larger ships was gone and with it a substantial amount of the meager food supplies.

Again Magellan had to make a decision. Again he decided that there was no turning back. The riches of the Orient were within reach. They must sail on to the Moluccas.

On the morning of November 28, 1520, the trio of little ships moved out of the strait onto the broad blue ocean which Magellan named the Pacific—the peaceful ocean.

12

The Pacific

PEACEFUL IT WAS, this vast expanse of water, sparkling under a cloudless sky—a beautiful change from the grim Atlantic and the barren fastness of the strait.

Magellan studied his charts. According to the mapmakers, the land mass of South America was separated from the East Indies only by a narrow band of ocean. A few days, a week of westward voyaging at most, and they would be at their destination.

However, they did not turn westward at once. The southern sun was bright, but it shed scant warmth. The men, suffering from months of winter weather, needed to rid their bones of chill. Magellan directed his helmsman to steer north, toward warmer waters, and the *Concepcion* and the *Victoria* fell in behind the *Trinidad*.

It was an unwise move, but Magellan did not know it then. Nor was there any way he could have known, although he might have suspected from recent experience that his charts were not entirely accurate. Given the state of navigational knowledge at the time, his mistake was not so much error as accident, but it was still to cost the expedition dearly.

Meanwhile they continued on, unaware. The three ships, borne by favorable winds, sped northward. The weather was fair and grew warmer each day. The men had caught fish and birds in the strait, so food was plentiful, though the fresh supplies had to be eaten quickly before they spoiled. The first week passed in comfort and optimism. Everyone, including Magellan, believed that the three ships would soon be loaded with a fabulous cargo of spices. The men had endured much suffering for the sake of these spices, but that was all in the past.

After several days, Magellan decided that they had sailed far enough due north, and he veered to a northwesterly course. He knew that the Moluccas lay astride the equator, and he calculated that the new course would bring him directly to the islands. Often during these days he spoke to his slave Enrique, cheerfully reminding him that he would soon be back in his native land, seeing his own people, speaking his own language. Not for one instant did the Captain General have any doubt that what he said was true.

Not the first week. Nor the second, nor even the third. But after nearly a month of sailing he began to wonder, only occasionally in the beginning, then more and more frequently. The fresh food was gone. Only biscuit remained. There had been little enough of that when they left the strait; now that the stores contained nothing else, it began to disappear with alarming speed. The men were not the only ones eating the biscuit ration. Scores of rats, growing ever bolder, gnawed their way into the chests containing the food and gorged themselves.

They could have managed, not well, but they could have managed if food had been the only problem. Water was a different matter. The heat was fierce, and it grew worse with each rising sun. Their supply of wine had long since been drunk. The water with which they had filled the casks the day before their departure from the *paso* had gone bad and was now crawling with ugly little worms. It stank, and the men gagged at the taste, but it was all they had. Every few days the fleet would run through a rain shower. Magellan would order the spare sails spread to catch what water they could, but the small amount obtained teased more than satisfied.

The men grew thin and irritable, then so weak that it was all they could do to carry out the simplest shipboard chore. They quarreled with one another unceasingly. There probably would have been murders had any of them been strong enough to pursue a brawl that far.

Another two weeks passed. Everyone aboard the three ships was covered with sores, partly from not having enough to eat, mainly because of the lack of fresh fruits and vegetables in their diet. Their teeth loosened and fell out. They retched and brought up blood.

And then they began to die. At first only a few, then more, until finally four or five men a day would succumb. Those who lived scarcely had the strength to carry their dead comrades to the rail and throw their bodies overboard to the sharks.

And still there was no sign of land, only the endless peaceful waters and the burning sun, the thin line of the horizon always before them like a cruel knife edge.

Pitched battles took place between men and rats. The rodents, teeth bared, eyes gleaming, would advance on the dead and the dying, intent on devouring their flesh. The men who could still stand would plunge after the rats, and if they caught one, would gather enough strength to strangle it. Then they would roast and eat it.

Soon there were no more rats left to appease the raging hunger of the men. They chewed on sawdust, which only increased their thirst. Then they ate the leather coverings of the mainyards. These were so hardened by years of exposure to sun and rain and wind that, before the men could eat them, they had to hang them overboard. Only after several days of soaking in the sea could the leather be cooked and wolfed down.

Magellan stood long hours on the quarterdeck of the *Trinidad*, narrowing his eyes toward the never-changing horizon, breaking his vigil only to go below and consult his charts. He now knew they were useless, but he kept studying them with desperate hope. One day, however, nearly two months since they had last seen land, he realized he could no longer place the slightest trust in the worthless bits of paper, nor use them to keep up his courage. He cast the charts aside.

That night he was more depressed than he had been at any other moment during the voyage. Even during the most dismal hours of searching for the *paso* he had not been so burdened with despair. Perhaps the sailors' yarns he had heard most of his life were true. Never before had he allowed himself to believe they might be, but now he wondered—perhaps this was the endless ocean of which he had been told. Perhaps it *would* happen that they would keep sailing, onward and onward, until they all died of starvation, and still the unmanned ships would continue to sail, into the setting sun, out of the rising sun, until the rotting vessels eventually fell apart and drifted as bits of debris on the vast surface of the ocean. Then finally even the pieces of planking and mast would rot, and there would be no trace ever again of the once-proud armada.

It was not a comforting thought.

In the darkness Magellan could hear the men—some groaning, others screeching with the shrill terror of insanity. Magellan himself was so weak he had difficulty standing upright, but he knew he had to.

But for how long?

Dawn began to brighten the eastern sky. Then, slowly, full day broke, and the sun rose. Already it was warm. It would become hotter, and the noonday sun would seem to hover forever over the three ships, threatening, waiting.

"Land—land ho!"

Magellan paid little attention to the voice. There were too many madmen aboard. In their madness they cried out at all hours of the day and night, voicing the dream of land which tortured their addled brains.

"Land ho!"

It was the lookout. Once before Magellan had believed a lookout to be mad, when the two ships he had thought were lost had returned from exploring the *paso*. That lookout turned out not to be insane, but this one surely was. In the past few weeks he had heard at least three of his men cry out in cracked voices from the crow's nest, shouting of land. He had watched them, still gibbering and screaming with horrible laughter, topple from their perch high on the mainmast into the sea. Their voices had grown silent then, and the razor-edged fins of the sharks had borne down on them, slicing through the blue water. The water boiled and bubbled briefly as the sharks squabbled over the bodies. . . .

"Land—land!"

Magellan did not even bother to look up. He continued to stare at the back of the helmsman, who in turn stared at nothing.

A cannon roared. Magellan turned. It was not one of the *Trinidad*'s guns. A puff of smoke rose from the *Concepcion*. There must be—what?

Only then did the Captain General direct his eyes up and ahead. He hardly dared believe what he saw. Many miles away, a lump on the thin horizon, rose the unmistakable shape of an island.

Now the men saw it. Those who could walk struggled to the most forward points of the ships and babbled among themselves, weeping and laughing at once. The sick and dying, unable to move from where they lay on the decks, cackled and sang bits of wild song.

Now at last there would be food. And water, blessed water. The ships sailed on, closer to the island. Its outline grew clearer.

Magellan, gazing through his own tears, wondered. Something was wrong—something. But the island was there. It was there, no disputing that. Something, though—

Then he understood. There were no trees. No trees meant little chance of fresh water, little chance of food. His despair returned, grew blacker as the *Trinidad* hove to and lay a few hundred yards off the clump of land.

The island was solid rock—white and grey and dappled rock. Not a sign of vegetation. Not a sign of life. Rock. It was worse, far worse, this disappointment, than not seeing land at all.

The rocks stirred, fluttered, took solid shape again. Magellan rubbed his eyes. Now he was going mad.

But once more he was sure he saw movement on the island. This time he forced himself to watch closely. He was not mistaken.

He cried out, so loudly that the helmsman turned to look at him. Of course—birds. The island was alive with birds.

Quickly he gathered a group of the strongest among the crew and sent them ashore in the skiff.

Aboard all three vessels everyone watched in silence as the landing party steered the skiff through the surf. If the birds flew away— But these creatures were not used to human beings and had no fear of them. The men seized them one after another, wrung their necks and tossed them into the skiff. Now boats were being lowered from the *Concepcion* and the *Victoria*.

That night there was food—roast fowl of all kinds.

But there was no water. And without water most of the men were able to choke down only a few morsels of food.

They were hardly better off than before. There was nothing to do but sail on, ever westward.

Magellan named this island, and another like it they saw soon after, Las Desaventuras—The Unfortunates. No one could challenge the aptness of the name.

It seems incredible, after all the suffering, then the brief hope followed by more suffering, that the men could endure more. Yet they did. They endured their privation for another five weeks. Single bright moments of fortune saved them. Several times there were violent downpours of rain; the water they caught in the sails kept them alive. One of the crew, trailing a fishline in the wake of the *Trinidad*, was able to hook a shark. It took the combined efforts of twenty men to bring it aboard, so weak had they grown. However, the shark flesh gave them the little extra strength they needed merely to survive.

Still, early in March of the year 1521, after a hundred days of sailing broken only by the momentary stop at the Unfortunate Islands, they were nearly defeated— three ships containing sick, ravaged men, all tottering on the brink of madness and death.

13

Full Circle

THERE WAS NOT even a lookout aloft on the morning of March 6. Magellan saw the island first. There was no enthusiasm in his voice as he spoke to the helmsman, no force in the words: "Steer over there."

Then he saw the trees. And there were huts as well. And people, men with light brown skins glistening in the sunlight as they crowded into canoes and paddled toward the *Trinidad.*

Magellan thought it was a dream. The others must have had the same thought. They stared dully at the agile brown figures climbing up the sides of the ship, swarming over the decks. The brown men chattered a great deal and laughed more.

Magellan soon realized what he was witnessing was no dream. The visitors were picking up everything within reach: buckets, nails, rope—everything they could lay hands on. One of the sailors tried to stop them. A tall native gave him a shove, and the weakened sailor fell to the deck and did not rise again.

The Captain General sensed that there was no malice in the thievery of the natives. European laws and values were not theirs. They saw something they wanted, and they simply took it. But they had to be stopped, or they would soon strip every scrap of equipment from the ship. Magellan called out an order to Espinosa, who was standing ready with his crossbow. The captain of the guard aimed an arrow at the native who had pushed the sailor. It struck him in the chest. He glanced down at it, tore it out of his body, looked at it in amazement, then touched his fingers to the blood gushing from the wound. His companions crowded around him, shaking their heads. It was obvious that none of them had ever seen a bow and arrow and regarded the weapon as something magic.

The man who had been hit crumpled to the deck, dead. The others gawked at him, then looked at their own weapons—frail wooden spears tipped with fishbone. They whispered rapidly among themselves, then, with quick, graceful movements slipped over the side of the ship and descended to their canoes.

In spite of their fear they were still able, before anyone could stop them, to cut the line securing the *Trinidad's* skiff to the ship. They paddled rapidly ashore, towing the small craft.

Magellan now faced another problem. He did not want to use violence against the natives. He had only ordered Espinosa to use his crossbow out of extreme necessity.

For one thing, he looked upon this island as a future Spanish province. Turning the inhabitants into enemies was not the best way to begin governing a land.

Nevertheless, the natives had stolen the flagship's skiff. Magellan did not intend to sail without it. Nor did he feel he could ask his men to continue the voyage without seeing that they received at least a taste of the food they knew to exist in abundance ashore.

He took no action that night. But mindful of the danger he and his men would be exposed to if they anchored close to shore, he conducted the fleet several miles out to sea, where they lay to until dawn.

As soon as the sun had risen, the *Trinidad* led the other two ships back into the bay where the island's village was located. The cannon ports were opened, and each ship fired a murderous broadside into the cluster of huts.

Magellan heard screams of pain and fear rising from the village. Then there was silence. He could see no one on the beach or among the huts. The Captain General was sick at heart over what he had done, but he felt there had been no choice. He led a landing party ashore.

The natives had evidently retreated into the hills, taking their dead and wounded with them. Magellan posted sentries at each entrance to the deserted village, then loaded his boats and the stolen skiff with casks of fresh water and with food: bananas, coconuts, chickens, and pigs. Then they returned to the ships, where everyone ate and drank as much as he could hold. Most of the men revived quickly, their long fast ended, but a number of them were too ill even to drink water, and they died.

Magellan named the island Ladrones, or Thieves'
Island. This name, too, like the one he had given to the
barren rock they had landed at five weeks before, was
apt—perhaps more apt than Magellan understood: each
side had had its turn at stealing.

The hunger of the surviving men satisfied, they sailed
on in more leisurely fashion, passing many islands now,
pausing to pick up food and water at some, but seeing
no more people until they stopped to rest at an island
which Pigafetta called Humunu. This was a tiny bit of
land, also uninhabited, but on the second day of their
stay, a sentry spied a canoe full of brown-skinned men
approaching the shore. Magellan, his memory of the
encounter at the Ladrones still fresh, cautioned his
soldiers to stand ready. But the visitors did not seem
hostile; they came across the beach toward the European
voyagers smiling and making friendly gestures. The Captain General relaxed a little, and asked Enrique to speak
to them. The men listened carefully to the slave's words,
but looked blank and made no reply.

Using sign language, Magellan inquired where they

The Ladrone Islands,
as drawn by
Antonio Pigafetta
in his diary

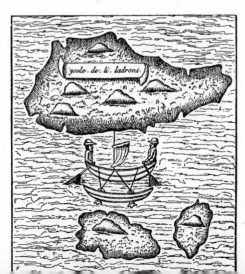

came from. They pointed to a large island some miles away and said over and over, "Suluan, Suluan."

Magellan was puzzled. He was under the impression that he had finally reached the Moluccas. But if this were true, Enrique and the men would have been able to converse. And in all the letters Magellan's blood brother Serrano had written, there had never been any mention of an island called Suluan.

We understand now that Magellan's mistake months before was responsible for what was taking place at this moment. He had sailed too far north along the coast of South America. The land he discovered was part of the great group of islands we presently call the Philippines. This territory was to become one of Spain's richest possessions and to remain under her rule for centuries, but at the time Magellan considered its discovery practically worthless.

It is just as well he did not realize the second consequence of his error. If he had not made the decision to turn north after leaving the *paso*, if he had sailed a direct course from South America to the Moluccas, not only would he have reached the fabled islands sooner, but he and his men would not have had to endure the agonies to which they had been exposed for so many weeks. The fleet would have come upon island after island, none more than a few days' journey from another, each one a source of food and water.

The error of ten degrees in navigation had very nearly proved fatal.

Yet, even after all the suffering, more than half the

men were still alive and well on the way to complete recovery. The ships, though badly in need of repair, could still be sailed. They could still be called an expedition, and they had not yet reached their goal.

Magellan ordered the armada under way and set a course to the south.

When they had been at sea two days, the fleet almost lost its keeper of records. Antonio Pigafetta, fishing over the side of the ship, slipped on a wet spar and tumbled into the water. The young Italian was unable to swim, and at first no one heard his cries. By incredible good fortune he managed to grab a rope dangling from the stern of the *Trinidad* and moments later was hauled aboard. Fortunate for us that he was, for without his careful diary entries we should have been without knowledge of the later events of the voyage.

Just before sunset on March 28, which happened to be the day before Good Friday, the three ships anchored off a large and lush-looking island. A flock of canoes put out from shore and were soon circling the ships. Enrique, watching idly from the deck of the Trinidad, called out a greeting in Malay. To his surprise and Magellan's delight, the men in the canoes answered. Soon a lively conversation was in progress.

Enrique discovered that the men did not speak exactly the same language as he, but it was close enough so they could understand one another. The expedition had not yet reached the Moluccas, but Enrique's homeland was obviously not too far away.

For Enrique there was merely the intense pleasure of speaking something like his own tongue again. But for Magellan the incident signified a triumph which he clearly understood and savored.

Men had said the earth was round. Most navigators of the time believed it, but no one until this very instant had proved it. The theory could never again be disputed.

An eighteenth-century map of the East Indies, showing the Philippines, the Moluccas (Moluques), Malacca, and the Ladrones (Marianes)

Full Circle

Twelve years before, Magellan had left the Orient and sailed westward. Now, after a long and harrowing journey, ever westward but broken at many stages, he had finally returned to his starting point.

Ferdinand Magellan and his slave Enrique had become the first men to make a complete voyage around the world.

Disaster

THEY FOUND OUT that the island where they were anchored was called Mazzava. The ruler proved as friendly
as his subjects who had come in their canoes to greet
the Spanish ships.

Magellan sent Enrique ashore, accompanied by Pigafetta, to act as his personal emissaries and, of course,
to represent the King of Spain. The two men took gifts
with them and were well received, almost too well received it would appear. The day was Good Friday. Pigafetta, a Catholic, had intended to fast but when the Rajah
of Mazzava invited him to sit down to a feast, the Italian
could not very well refuse. Pigafetta and Enrique ate
heartily from huge platters of steamed pork, vegetables,
bananas, and coconuts. They also drank great quantities
of strong palm wine.

And then, to their dismay, the moment they had finished eating, the rajah's chieftains insisted that the two guests come with them for a second banquet.

One feast was enough. Two would have been just bearable. But when they had eaten as much as they could of the second meal, the rajah's son arrived. He was not to be outdone by his father's chieftains in offering hospitality to the foreigners. Pigafetta and Enrique had to eat and drink their way through a third enormous repast. They managed to do it, but then were unable to get up from the cane mats on which they were sitting. To the great delight of all the onlookers, the two guests toppled over and at once fell asleep.

It was noon the next day before they felt steady enough on their feet to return to their ship. Pigafetta went immediately to the priest. He had to confess that, not only had he broken a holy fast, but he had been guilty of the sin of gluttony as well. However, he pointed out, it was all in the service of the Lord, since he hoped that the friendly encounter would help bring Christianity to these charming pagans. What Pigafetta omitted saying was that he had completely enjoyed the experience.

After this, it was fitting that the rajah visit Magellan aboard the *Trinidad*. The ruler of Mazzava was impressed by the stern Captain General, who could also be warm and likeable when he chose, as he did now. With Enrique acting as interpreter, the two men talked for hours. Out of this conversation came the information that Mazzava was not the principal island in the region. Cebu was much larger and more important, ruled over by a wise and powerful rajah named Humabon. The Rajah of Mazzava offered to guide Magellan's fleet to Cebu.

The journey took three days, at the end of which the armada dropped anchor in a busy harbor crammed with vessels of all shapes and sizes: Arab dhows, Chinese junks, and a multitude of native canoes.

Once again, the Captain General decided to send Enrique and Pigafetta ashore as his envoys. Because of the trading activity at the harbor, Magellan suspected that the ruler with whom they would be dealing now would be much more a man of the world than any they had met on the voyage thus far. Therefore he gave his slave detailed instructions as to how he should conduct the mission.

Ashore, in the royal palace, the two ambassadors found themselves in the presence of a squat, shrewd-looking man clad only in a loin cloth and a richly jeweled turban. Tattoo designs in a variety of colors covered his limbs, chest, and back. He was eating a mixture of spicy-smelling foods off delicate porcelain dishes.

This was the Rajah Humabon.

He welcomed Pigafetta and Enrique cordially and invited them to be seated. He offered them food and drink, but they were aware that he was watching them carefully, making up his mind about them. For a time, while they ate, Humabon was silent. Eventually he said, "You and your master, the man Magellan of whom you speak, and all those who sail the ships which have come from so great a distance, may consider Cebu your home for as long as you wish to remain. You will be able to trade freely with us. We demand from you only that you pay the customary tribute fees into the treasury of our land."

Enrique, having been instructed by Magellan, was waiting for this. "What you suggest is impossible," he replied. "My master serves the ruler of Spain and no other. King Charles pays neither fees no duties."

Humabon frowned. He clapped his hands. A number of armed warriors appeared. Pigafetta was alarmed, certain that he and Enrique would be arrested and sent to languish in some airless dungeon. He waited, wondering how to signal Enrique to leap to his feet and join him in an attempt to escape.

The rajah whispered a few words to one of the soldiers. The man nodded and went out of the chamber. Other soldiers stationed themselves in front of the exits from the throne room. Pigafetta sighed, giving up his idea of flight.

After a time the soldier reappeared. With him was an Arab, who walked toward the rajah, stopped before him, and bowed until his forehead touched the floor.

"This man," said Humabon, "also comes from far away. He is a wealthy merchant who owns many ships. He has visited Cebu many times and enjoys a profitable trade with us. When he comes, he pays without question the tribute we ask." He then addressed the Arab. "Is this not so?"

The Arab rose and for the first time looked at Pigafetta and Enrique. He started to speak but faltered after a word or two. Then he approached Humabon and whispered, though loud enough for Enrique to hear and understand the Malay words. "Excellency," he said, "I know the place from which these men come. They are ruthless warriors. They possess mighty weapons. If they become displeased—" He left the sentence hanging.

Enrique said quickly, "The King of Spain is a man of peace. My master, who serves him, has no wish to make war. His only desire is to come and go freely, and to trade, so that you and he may each grow richer as a result of his visits." He paused. "But if he is indeed made angry—" As had the Arab, Enrique left his speech unfinished.

The warriors shuffled their feet and moved closer to Humabon, watching his face for some sign that they should act. Pigafetta began to despair again, certain he would never leave the room alive.

Humabon sat blinking at the two emissaries. Slowly he raised a porcelain cup to his lips and took a swallow of wine. Then he smiled. "We shall trade," he said.

Nothing more was mentioned about tributes or harbor fees.

Magellan came ashore. He and Humabon exchanged formal greetings. Then their conversation became more friendly. Late in the evening Magellan showed the rajah the bars of iron he had brought as a gift. Humabon thanked him politely. The Captain General then brought out several vases of Venetian glass. Humabon once more thanked him and set the vases beside the iron. But Magellan noticed that Humabon kept looking at the iron bars. The rajah's eyes glittered. He started to put out his hand to touch the iron, saw Magellan watching him, and drew his hand back quickly. Then Humabon ordered a large box brought into the throne room. He opened it. Inside lay ingots of pure gold. "For you," he said to Magellan.

The Captain General gazed at the yellow metal gleaming under the torchlight. It was worth a small fortune. "Thank you," he said, "but I should really prefer the porcelain cup in which you have served me wine."

Humabon stared at Magellan for a moment. Then he said, "It shall be as you wish."

Magellan cautiously let out the breath he had been holding. He longed to take the gold, all of it he could lay hands on. But he was sure that Humabon was a clever bargainer. Even though the rajah obviously wanted iron badly, Magellan knew that if he once sensed that gold was precious to the Europeans, the price would climb out of sight.

The show of restraint worked. From that moment on, Magellan allowed Humabon to force gold upon him, giving the rajah only an equal weight of iron in return. In actual fact, each man gained and neither lost. Each gave something of little value to himself and received something he prized greatly. The basis for trade was now set.

But gold was not the only treasure the expedition hoped to take back. To the south lay the Moluccas and an immense supply of spices. Other Spanish captains could return to Cebu and trade iron for more gold.

There remained one more task for Magellan to accomplish before leaving Cebu. When he set out from Spain, the Captain General had pledged to the Church, as did all leaders of expeditions departing for strange lands, that he would convert as many of the natives as possible to the Christian religion.

He and the priests aboard the ships spent many hours talking about conversion with Humabon. The rajah was attracted to the idea. "You must not," Magellan warned him, "become a Christian to please me. If you should

The baptism of the Rajah Humabon

decide not to, no one will harm you, or think ill of you. But of course if you do adopt our religion, it will make the ties between us so much stronger. . . ."

Humabon made his decision. He and all his people would be baptized. The rites took place the following Sunday. So many converts appeared before the priests that by the end of the day they were too exhausted even to raise their arms in blessing. The mass baptisms continued for almost a week. A cross was erected at the main entrance to the rajah's palace, signifying that the inhabitants of Cebu were now good Christians.

Magellan's task was finished. He was ready now to sail for the Moluccas. If he had done so at once, all might have gone well. But Magellan was anxious to prove to Humabon that the rajah had done the right thing by allowing the Spaniards to trade freely and by accepting Christianity for himself and his people. He questioned the rajah: was there nothing the Spanish fleet could do for Cebu, no service large or small which Magellan could personally perform? Humabon shook his head. The Captain General persisted. Had the people of Cebu no enemies?

Humabon's eyes brightened. As a matter of fact, he replied, there was an enemy, not one of great strength, but an enemy nonetheless. The neighboring isle of Mactan was in revolt against the rule of Cebu. Humabon had long been planning to send a force to put down the rebellion.

Magellan knew Mactan. During their stay at Cebu, some Spaniards had visited the island. There had been trouble between the natives and the Europeans. At least part of the difficulty had probably been caused by the sailors' sudden fondness for the local ladies, but Magellan did not take this into particular account. His new brothers, the people of Cebu, had named an enemy. Magellan had no reason to feel friendly toward the inhabitants of Mactan. He would therefore show the rajah of Cebu the full glory and might of Spain.

The Captain General was not a bloodthirsty man. His intention was only to subdue Mactan with a show of strength. He sent Enrique to the chieftain of Mactan, demanding that he surrender and spare his people from the massacre which would take place if he did not.

Magellan was confident that there would be no battle. But Silapulapa, the chieftain of Mactan, was a proud and stubborn man. He replied that he and his warriors would defend their island to the death.

If there had been some way of withdrawing gracefully at this point, Magellan might have done so. But he had told the Rajah of Cebu that he would conquer Mactan. The honor of Spain was at stake. Still, the Captain General had no desire to initiate a mass slaughter. He was certain that the sight of a few men wearing European armor and equipped with European weapons would strike enough fear in the hearts of the simple natives to make them flee into the hills.

He refused Humabon's offer of a thousand men. He

rejected the suggestion of Serrano and Duarte Barbosa that the three ships open fire on Mactan with their cannons. He would not even take his entire fighting force with him on the venture. He chose sixty men for the attack, planning to lead them himself. Magellan believed that a few rounds of musket fire, a few arrows loosed from crossbows, at the most, would result in a quick victory for the Spanish.

The sixty men set out just before dawn in three long-boats. Fifteen hundred Mactan warriors stood on the sandy shore, awaiting their approach. The natives were armed only with flimsy bows and arrows and with wooden spears, the tips of which had been hardened in fire.

The boats drove steadily shoreward. Suddenly there was a grinding sound under the hull of the lead craft, and its forward motion ceased. It had run onto a reef. The other two boats tried to detour around the reef, but it was too large. Moments later all three boats were stuck fast, unable to get closer to shore.

Magellan removed his leg armor and leaped into the water, which was only waist-deep at that point. He ordered forty soldiers to follow him, leaving twenty in the boats.

It was broad daylight now. The natives on the shore stood in silence as the Spaniards waded toward them. Now the men in the boats opened fire with muskets and crossbows. The Mactan ranks wavered, frightened by the noise of gunfire. But the distance was too great. The bullets and arrows either fell short or inflicted only very slight wounds on the natives. The chieftain Silapulapa shouted a command. The lines of Mactan warriors straightened and held. They no longer feared the European weapons.

Magellan's landing party now began to fire, but the men had not yet gained the shore. It was difficult enough to keep their footing on the slippery bottom, much less handle the awkward crossbows. The warriors of Mactan charged shrieking into the sea, loosing poisoned arrows, hurling their wooden spears. They soon singled out Magellan, concentrating their attack on him. And as they drew closer, they perceived he was not wearing leg armor. A score of arrows streaked toward the Captain General. One imbedded itself in his lame leg. Magellan pulled it out, stumbled to his knees, rose again. Realizing that his force was not only badly outnumbered but in an impossible position, he gave the order for a slow and steady retreat.

The Mactan warriors, having drawn blood, pressed their advantage. They swarmed toward the Spaniards and engaged them in close fighting. Twice, Magellan's helmet was knocked off. Twice he managed to retrieve it. An arrow wounded him in the right arm. He shifted his lance to his left hand and thrust it into the chest of an onrushing Mactan. The man fell, taking Magellan's lance with him. Magellan tried to draw his sword, but his right arm was now useless. The enemy was upon him. Pigafetta, battling furiously a few yards away, made a heroic

The battle of Mactan

effort to reach his captain, but found himself driven even farther away, back toward the boats.

A dozen Mactan warriors seized Magellan, forced him under the water, and struck at him again and again with their spears. Then they stopped, and remained quietly looking down, weapons dangling from their hands. The surface of the water was still. Pigafetta, watching helplessly from a distance, knew it was over.

Magellan was dead.

15

The Voyage Home

WHEN AN EXPEDITION loses its leader, no one is exactly sure what will happen. Sometimes a new leader arises, even stronger than the old, and takes command at once, restoring the courage and faith of the men. Such was not the case with the Spanish armada.

Magellan had many faults. He was proud, often unreasonable, given to somber moods and fits of temper. His judgment was not always perfect. As we have seen, he made many errors which came close to destroying the fleet. But he was strong. When he gave a command, it was obeyed, and those who opposed him usually regretted it. He was ambitious, but his first consideration was the welfare of his men. True, he led them time after time into agonizing situations, but he was always ready to work as hard as the lowest seamen, and their suffering was also his. Some of the men might have hated him; all respected him. In short, he was a highly capable leader.

After Magellan's death, Duarte Barbosa was elected Captain General. He was young, and though he had a certain amount of experience, he was not up to taking charge of the weary and unhappy Spanish armada.

Nor had Magellan left him an easy command. The three ships, veterans of many months of sea time, were beginning to leak badly. There was scarcely enough crew to man them properly. Also, the expedition's disastrous defeat at the hands of the Mactan warriors had caused the friendly Humabon to have doubts about the value of being allied with the Spaniards.

Still, if Magellan had lived, he probably could have saved the situation. With all his faults, he was an impressive man. It is likely he could have persuaded the Rajah of Cebu to remain friendly.

As it was, Humabon did not trust Duarte Barbosa. Moreover, Silapulapa, chieftain of Mactan, was now a powerful man as a result of his victory over the white men. He told Humabon to join forces with him or he would pull him off his throne. Humabon had no choice. He sat with Silapulapa and plotted treachery against the Spaniards.

Barbosa suspected nothing. Humabon invited him and Juan Serrano to a feast. The two officers went, together with a number of men from the armada. When the Spaniards had drunk enough palm wine to rob them of their ability to fight, Humabon ordered his warriors to slaughter them. Barbosa was killed at once, Serrano a short while later.

The fleet of course had to leave Cebu in great haste. A pilot by the name of Carvalho took over as Captain General. His first act, as soon as the ships were far enough away from Cebu, was to declare the *Concepcion* unseaworthy. Her crew and equipment were transferred to the *Trinidad* and the *Victoria*. Then she was burned and sunk. The other two ships proceeded southward in the direction of the Moluccas.

Carvalho was not a skillful pilot. He led the ships on a wandering course, and it soon became apparent he had not the slightest idea where he was going. As a matter of fact, he was more interested in robbing other ships, drinking, and brawling than in reaching the Spice Islands. The other officers tired of his command, voted to remove him, and in his place set Espinosa, who had been Magellan's captain of the guard. Espinosa knew nothing of navigation, but he had the good sense to move cautiously from island to island and to make inquiries at each one from local seafarers. In time, what was left of the fleet reached the Moluccas.

Unfortunate news awaited them. The island of Ternate, where Magellan's cousin Francisco Serrano had been living, was in the hands of the Portuguese. The king had been poisoned, and Serrano, because he was the king's friend, had also been murdered by his own countrymen.

Espinosa quickly ordered his ships away from the danger area. A few days later the Spanish luck changed.

They discovered another island, even more abundant in spices than Ternate. They were able to take on a fantastically rich cargo in a matter of a few days. Then they started back for Spain.

The old *Trinidad* was not able to make it. Her timbers were rotten, her pumps practically useless against the water pouring in through the split seams of her hull. She returned to the Moluccas, where she was captured by the Portuguese. Her commander, Espinosa, was imprisoned.

The *Victoria,* captained by Sebastian del Cano, a former pilot, struggled on toward Europe. Her voyage was nearly as difficult as the one she had made across the Pacific in the company of her sister ships. Now she was sailing through well-charted waters, but this did not help her. She passed the tip of India and headed for the African coast. Her plight was desperate. All the coastal cities were in Portuguese hands. To stop at any of them for food and water meant sure capture. The *Victoria* stayed well out to sea. Her crew came close to starving and dying of thirst. Yet during the entire voyage, weak as he grew, Antonio Pigafetta wrote each day in his journal, setting down everything he saw and heard.

Finally, on September 8, 1522, three years after they had set out, the *Victoria's* crew sailed the little ship up the Guadalquiver River and let go the anchor in the harbor of Seville.

The whole population of the city turned out to welcome them. Not only had they brought back a cargo of incredible value, enough to pay all the expenses of the expedition several times over; they had sailed on one voyage completely around the earth. They were heroes.

The crew of the *Victoria* did not feel heroic. Several hundred men had embarked on the expedition. Eighteen ill and exhausted men staggered off the battered galleon and kissed the soil of Spain.

Pigafetta stood apart, listening to the roar of the welcoming crowd, watching the wealthy merchants strain forward to touch the men who had just made them even richer.

The young Italian felt only sadness and a great lonely longing for his friend the stern-eyed captain who had made all this happen. It had been Magellan's dream which had started others dreaming, Magellan's drive which had kept the expedition moving onward through peril and doubt.

Now they were back. And the man who should have been there to take credit for the exploit lay dead, his body rotting on a tiny island thousands of miles from Spain.

Pigafetta turned away and wept.

THE VICTORIA

Pigafetta presenting his history of the voyage to the Spanish King Charles

Chronology of Magellan's Life

1480	Birth in Portugal, near Lisbon
1495–1505	Serves as apprentice seaman, then junior officer, in Portuguese navy
1505–1510	Serves on ships in East Indies
1511–1514	Promoted to ship's captain; continues to sail in East Indies
1515–1516	Fights with Portuguese army in Morocco

Chronology of Magellan's Life

Spring, 1517	Audience with King Manuel in Lisbon
October 20, 1517	Arrives in Seville
March 22, 1518	Charter for expedition to the Moluccas signed by King Charles of Spain
September 20, 1519	Fleet sails from Spain
December 13, 1519	Arrival in Rio
January 11, 1520	Fleet reaches false *paso*
March 31, 1520	Arrival at winter quarters, San Julian
April 1, 1520	Mutiny in San Julian
May 22, 1520	*Santiago* lost on exploration trip
August 24, 1520	Departure from San Julian for Santa Cruz
October 21, 1520	Fleet reaches entrance to *paso*
November 8, 1520	*San Antonio* deserts
November 28, 1520	Fleet enters the Pacific
March 6, 1521	Fleet reaches the Ladrone Islands
March 16, 1521	Fleet reaches the Philippines
March 28, 1521	Anchorage at Mazzava. Enrique speaks with natives; Magellan realizes he has circled the world.
April 27, 1521	Magellan killed in battle at Mactan

September 8, 1522	Sole surviving ship of the fleet, the *Victoria*, reaches Seville and becomes first vessel in history to circumnavigate the earth on a single voyage.

153

Picture Credits: